MARIJUANA

❦ OUTDOORS ❦

GUERILLA
GROWING

by Jorge Cervantes

Many anonymous people (you know who you are) provided valuable input and support to make this book possible....Thanks!

Published in the USA, Spain, Germany
Copyright 2000 by GVP
9 8 7 6 5 4 3 2
ISBN-13: 978-1-878823-28-1
ISBN-10: 1-87883-28-0

Editors: Jordi Bricker, Soledad Coyote, Jose T. Gallego, Annie Rieken
Art work: R. Nightingale, Sergey Shmat
Photos: Jorge Cervantes, Canamo Lectores, G. Curtis, Goyum
Cover Photo: Goyum
Book & Cover Design, Color Section: Chris Thompson

For wholesale orders, please contact:

North America: Homestead Books:
www.homesteadbook.com, 1-800-426-6777

North America: Quick Distribution: 1-510-527-7036

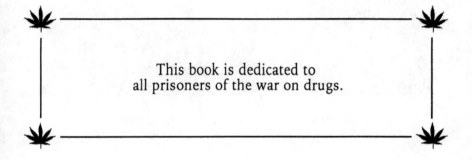

This book is dedicated to
all prisoners of the war on drugs.

James Cox
11952 San Andres Dr.
St. Louis, MO 63138

 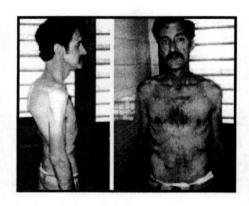

Left photo: James with his family in better times.
Right photo: James suffered from severe weight loss following his
incarceration and prior to the surgeries.

Cancer and radiation poisoning patient James Cox age 50, sentenced to 15 years; served 5 with 10 years probation, charged with medical marijuana cultivation.

James Cox was introduced to medical marijuana following two operations for testicular cancer that had metastasized to his stomach. He found that it helped his pain, nausea, and eating disorders resulting from the cancer, chemotherapy and radiation therapy.

During his illness he was prescribed the narcotic, Demerol, which, in combination with marijuana, helped him cope with chronic pain from the nerve damage to his stomach, other organs, and ulcers. Marijuana also helped his inability to tolerate food and loss of appetite. James was on Demerol for fifteen years and became addicted. He found that if he increased his marijuana intake he could get off the debilitating Demerol and gain control of his life.

Since James could not afford to buy his marijuana medicine on the black market, he began to grow his own. Police discovered his garden while investigating an attempted burglary to his home. James and his wife, Pat, were arrested and the home they had just inherited from her mother was confiscated. James was sentenced to fifteen years behind bars, and Pat to five. Devastated and depressed, they attempted suicide while out on bond, but were discovered and saved. His sentence was given a stay and they were sent home. A free man, James' desire to live returned, and he went back to growing his medicine. His health improved, but two years later, James was arrested once again on cultivation charges. This time they locked him away.

Lacking adequate medical attention in prison, he was near death. It took two stomach surgeries during his incarceration to keep him alive.

"Since I have been incarcerated and deprived of its use, I have lived in constant discomfort which I feel is a direct result of not having the medical benefits of marijuana. My stomach deteriorated to the point to where I could not eat anything due to incurable bleeding ulcers," James wrote in 1995.

After spending almost five years in prison, James has finally gone home, but his government-enforced suffering is not over yet. James pain is intolerable and doctors concur with this. However, he will be on parole for the next ten years and will be drug tested twice a week for marijuana for the next three years. Doctors can, however, prescribe morphine for him. As a result, he has tested positive for opiate-type drugs. The state of Missouri is now threatening to send this patient back to prison for medicating his pain to bring it to a tolerable threshold.

MARIJUANA OUTDOORS: **GUERILLA GROWING**

Table of Contents

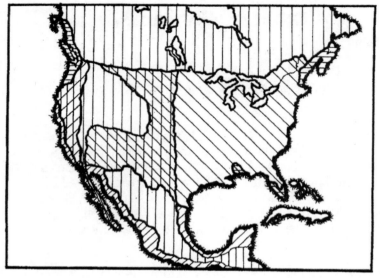

**Climatic Zones of
North America
and
Europe**

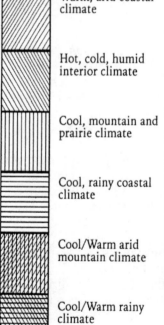

Warm, arid coastal
climate

Hot, cold, humid
interior climate

Cool, mountain and
prairie climate

Cool, rainy coastal
climate

Cool/Warm arid
mountain climate

Cool/Warm rainy
climate

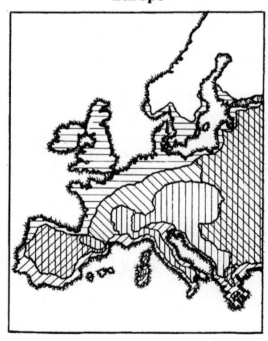

Introduction

Marijuana Outdoors: Guerilla Growing shows readers how marijuana growers in diverse climates on several continents use guerilla (clandestine) gardening techniques to grow the absolute best marijuana with the help of Mother Nature. Worldwide, more and more high quality marijuana is grown outdoors every year. Growers in North America, Central and Western Europe, Australia and New Zealand are applying the simple principles reported in this book to grow more and better marijuana every day. From the many growers in each climate, one "composite" grower was created to illustrate gardening in that area. We examine four major *cannabis* growing climates starting with a short chapter on the basics. Composite growers from different climates demonstrate the simple step-by-step examples and explain exactly how they grow great crops.

Hundreds of growers were interviewed to collect information for this book. The composite growers that are profiled are from five completely different climates. A special short section on drought gardening is also included. Different climates require different growing techniques and strategies. Each of the examples gives you a personal look at the climate and specific challenges they face. For example, a grower in the mountains of Switzerland or the Rocky Mountains of North America employs much different growing techniques than a grower in an arid desert climate on Spain's Iberian Peninsula or coastal California. Yet, both growers are cultivating the same plant and may use many similar techniques. To completely understand one climate, readers must study all climates in this book because it focuses on the similarities and differences between these growers and their climates. The detailed Appendix and Index will help define terms and prove invaluable to serious readers.

Each chapter starts with a brief introduction of the growers, climate and growing situation. All the growers profiled have the same desire: to grow top quality marijuana safely, easily and invest as little work and money as possible. The tour continues by outlining their garden site selection and preparation in relation to security. Climate and soil are the main focus of each chapter because they dictate what the growers need to do to achieve the best results.

Solutions to growing problems may vary from climate to climate, but could be the same too. Adequate water may be the main concern in a dry climate and protection from cool weather in a mountain climate. Bud mold may be the main concern in moist climates regardless of their elevation or location.

Growers also use a combination of indoor and outdoor gardening to achieve the most secure results. With the advent of numerous seed companies supplying excellent seed stock, growers can cultivate clones indoors and move them outdoors to increase harvest and lower work load.

Guerilla growers also give numerous cultivation tips that are highlighted as dialogue. One editor commented: "Reading each chapter is like talking to a friend that has grown marijuana in my climate for the last 20 years. They can tell you everything they did, beginning to end, and best of all, it's real, right-on advice".

The Appendix is packed with information on *cannabis*, soil, fertilizers, water, insects and more.

Watch for my articles in *Cannabis Culture* (Canada), *High Times* (US) *Hanf, Grow* (Germany), *HighLife, Essensie* (Netherlands), *Weed World, Red Eye Express* (UK), *Canamo, El Cogollo, Mundo High* (Spain) and hit our web site -

http://marijuanagrowing.com

- It is packed with pages and pages of current information about growing. We post new information regularly. Also, read other garden magazines and the gardening section in your local newspaper for more information on your local climate.

Conversations with a Great Guerilla Grower

Tom, an American, is one of the most successful growers I have ever interviewed. His methods are extremely simple and easy. He is a smart, lazy man who pays attention to Mother Nature. Tom's complete and simple understanding of plant growth makes him a very successful guerilla grower. These simple concepts are key to assimilating guerilla growing.

Wild marijuana plants are vigorous, aggressive, competitive weeds. Some varieties have a large root system which helps them survive moisture stress and poor soil. Plants spaced at least 10 feet apart will grow to a height of 3 - 5 feet in dry climates. Cannabis is a survivor. Given control of a growing area of 4 to 12 square feet, in poor soil, mature plants will grow to about 5 feet tall with a strong terminal main bud or cola. The yield is relatively heavy considering the amount of cultivation work. Add a little more effort during soil preparation and planting to grow several times more dope. Loosen the soil, amend it a little and throw in a handful of polymers*. Cover the soil around the plant with a thick layer of natural mulch to attract condensed water and to keep soil moisture from evaporating. Just these simple measures may double the yield.

Reasonable soil will grow a plant that is 7 – 8 feet tall with roots that spread 5 feet across and 6 feet deep. This plant will yield 2 – 10 times more marijuana than if planted in poor soil.

To prepare an outdoor garden, remove the weeds in the fall, dig planting holes and prepare the soil. The soil will absorb rainfall and be well mixed the next spring. Cover each planting hole with a layer of mulch to protect it from winter rains and temperatures. This layer of mulch is very important. Do not leave soil bare all winter.

Transplant seedlings or clones in spring and grow marijuana plants as you would tomatoes. If growing in poor soil, give each plant a hole that is 4 feet deep and 4 feet in diameter and refill with your best compost/potting soil/planting mix. Break up the soil in a wide 6-foot radius, only 6 - 8 inches deep, because roots branch out.

To water cheaply and effectively, cut a 3/16th hole in the bottom of a 5-gallon bucket. Mix an inexpensive all purpose water-soluble fertilizer with 5-gallons of water in the bucket and put the hole by the stem of the plant. Growing like this, only with 4 - 6 buckets of water will last all summer. Water with one bucket every 10 days

*polymer crystals are small crystals that expand to about 15 times their size when moistened by water. They are added to soil to prolong time between watering.

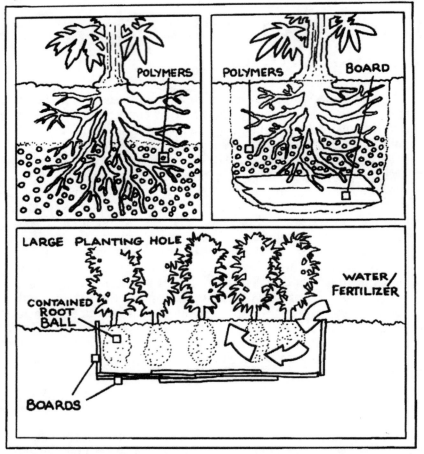

Polymer crystals hold water and gradually release it as the soil dries out. Polymer crystals cut watering frequency dramatically.

during hot weather. Watering with this regimen, the plants will grow as well as if they had lots of water.

If plants receive no water, a small bud grows on top of plant. A 5 foot tall plant may produce from 1 - 6 ounces of smokable bud. This same plant, given just a little water, will grow much better and produce more high quality smoke.

Grow a plant that takes 20 – 40 gallons of supplemental water per growing season, or grow a plant that gets an infinite amount of water and achieve very near the same weight at harvest. Why?

First the plant must use all water in the soil. The plant must get all the nutrients it needs that naturally occur in the subsoil. If you slightly increase the water and nutrient supply, you get a much stronger and robust plant.

How much water is there in the soil already? Reasonable soil has one inch of water per foot of area. There are about 30 gallons of water already in the soil in 4 x 4 x 4-feet area of reasonable soil.

To plant in the country, look for big green stands of vegetation. Kill green vegetation in the fall and grow the garden the following spring. One of the main things to look for is an adequate water supply. Many parts of the US and different parts of the world get rainfall in the summer growing season to support a dry land crop. The rainfall you need is from ¼ to 1 inch per week. It is very important that it rains regularly during the spring and summer months. Dry fall weather is the best for harvests. Heavy rains and high humidity will cause bud mold.

MARIJUANA OUTDOORS: **GUERILLA GROWING**

Cool, Rainy Coastal Climate
NW USA, BC, Canada, UK, Coastal Europe

Introduction

Vansterdan lives on the lower mainland, British Columbia, in Canada's "Banana Belt", a climate blessed with moderate temperatures, an abundance of rain and evergreen conifer forests. Marijuana thrives in BC back yards. Garden patches in mountains and swamps demand little attention after planting. This climate is similar to that of the United Kingdom, Northern and Atlantic coastal Europe, Tasmania and southern New Zealand. Annual rainfall is 40 inches or more and winter comes early with low light levels and chilling rain that fosters rampant fungus growth.

Vansterdan has a large south-facing back yard enclosed by a high fence. He integrates his indoor grow room, outdoor greenhouse and garden for maximum production. He starts clones under lights and moves them outdoors into a small heated greenhouse, backyard and mountain gardens.

Last year Vansterdan purchased seeds from Dutch and Canadian seed companies. He took 30 clones from each of the following mother plants: 'Skunk #1', 'Jack Herer', 'Blueberry', 'Romulan', 'El Nino' and 'Super Silver Haze', a total of 180 clones. Three weeks later, all 180 clones were well-rooted. Vansterdan chose the strongest half of each variety to move to his greenhouse and outdoor gardens.

He moved 30 clones into the backyard, 10 into the greenhouse and the remaining 50 he transplanted into patches in the nearby mountains.

Site/Security Selection

Security is a small issue in Vancouver. Vansterdan lives in a conservative neighborhood with neighbors on three sides. Plants can grow to the top of the back yard fence without detection. His greenhouse, located along the southern side of the house, measures 3 x 6 feet and is 4 feet tall. He grows 30 marijuana plants in the greenhouse and backyard among the vegetables. Some grow in the ground, others are kept in pots buried in the ground.

Vansterdan bought a Ministry of Forestry map of sectors near Vancouver, jumped on his mountain bike and set out to find new garden turf. His criteria: sunshine, limited public access and good water supply.

"I look for a south-facing hillside where the sun shines all day long, aye. The forest provides good cover for secrecy but the tall trees make too much shade. That's why I look for stands of thorny blackberries, ferns or meadow grass to plant," said Vansterdan with a pronounced Canadian accent, zipping up his rain suit.

Security and site selection are easy in BC. There are few aerial patrols looking for marijuana and the countryside is green all year long, which makes marijuana difficult to distinguish from other foliage. Hikers, fishermen and hunters present the biggest security risk. Other similar climates in northern and coastal Europe are more populated and require more clandestine planting methods. Camouflaging the garden along a fence or among other plants is necessary. In BC, the primary obstacles are cool, wet weather and invasive foliage.

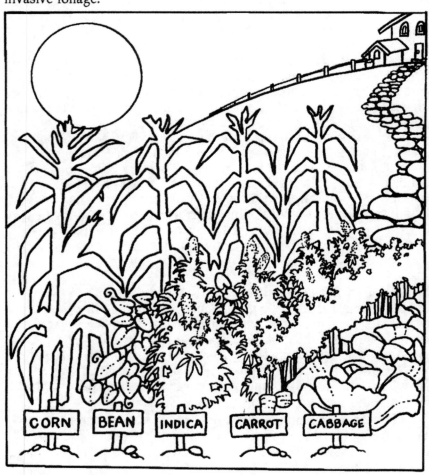

Marijuana blends and is camouflaged by many different back yard plants. Look for plants with similar leaf shapes that grow fast.

CHAPTER TWO

Site Preparation and Soil

Preparing three sites required three different strategies. The small greenhouse needs a little bit of heat to speed growth. Easy ways to warm a greenhouse include natural heat generated by the sun and artificial heat from electricity or burning fossil fuel. To conserve the natural heat from the sun, Vansterdan lined the bottom of the greenhouse with two inches of Styrofoam. He also placed a one-inch-thick lining six inches high around the bottom perimeter of the greenhouse. He constructed the greenhouse from Filon, a corrugated, translucent fiberglass. The low-slung greenhouse looks like a small storage area because you can't see inside. Filon transmits enough light for vegetative growth even when low levels of natural sunlight are available. To add more heat, Vansterdan used duct tape to fasten heating cable to the Styrofoam floor and covered it with a thin piece of sheet metal to transmit the heat evenly.

Vansterdan is an avid vegetable gardener and has been adding manure and compost to the raised beds in his backyard garden for more than 10 years. His neighbors are used to his fanatic gardening and do not suspect him of growing marijuana. Every spring he spreads three cubic yards of finished compost and manure over the garden. He adds dolomite lime to raise and stabilize the acidic pH and rototills it into the soil. Once vegetables are planted and growing well, Vansterdan transplants hardened-off clones into the garden plot.

"The soil is so rich and fertile, I don't even need a shovel to dig a planting hole. I just open the soil with my hand, put the clone in and press soil around the root ball before watering it in" said Vansterdan with the pride of a confirmed organic gardener.

Raised Beds

The soil in cool coastal regions is heavy clay that warms slowly and drains poorly. Raised beds turn both of these detriments into compliments. Beds need to be raised 6 – 8 inches to provide the benefits of warmth and improved drainage. Using raised beds, Vansterdan plants from two weeks to a month earlier than other gardeners.

If poor drainage is the only obstacle and making raised beds too difficult because of a remote garden location, smart growers loosen clay soils with a pick and shovel before cultivating in granulated gypsum to break up clay soil.

Compost

The basics of composting are simple: collect organic matter: grass clippings, chopped up branches and vegetative matter, pile it up and let it rot. The pile must be at least one yard square to hold more heat than is dissipated.

"It's easy to make compost," said Vansterdan. "In the summer, professional gardeners cut grass and other yard debris and haul it away. I asked one of them to dump the debris at the end of my driveway. He gives me about three cubic yards a week. By the end of the summer, I have more than 40 yards of grass clippings and garden debris. I mix it with wood chips to provide carbon and air. The following year, I have 3 to 6 cubic yards of the best compost in the world!"

"I know one hard core grower that plants spring crops on top of compost piles. He piles the compost up two or three feet high, making a raised bed. Next he throws 3 or 4 inches of good dirt on top and plants foot-tall clones, aye. By the time the roots penetrate down into the compost, it has cooled down and doesn't burn. The compost keeps the clones warm and he puts a greenhouse on top to protect the foliage. If he's lucky and the weather cooperates, he harvests a spring crop," said Vansterdan with a bewildered grin.

Mountain and Bog Soil

"Most of the soil around here is full of Douglas fir needles and is very acidic. The pH is around 5, which makes plants grow slowly, aye. I look for patches where pasture grass grows. The soil is normally a little poor, lacking nutrients, so I have two strategies. The first one, I use for low lying areas. To plant in marshy, grassy areas, I cut a square yard of moist sod from the ground with a shovel, turn it over, and plant in it. This way I can transplant about 50 clones in a day. The marshy ground supplies enough water and I just add a bit of time-release fertilizer when I transplant, aye. I add another handful of flowering time-release fertilizer when I go back and check them the first week in August. Sure, the plants don't grow as big as the ones in my back yard, but I don't work too hard, aye."

Vansterdan has been planting in the mountains for 12 years in secret gardens only accessible by foot or mountain bike. He harvests about half of the clones he plants. The rest are lost to humans and other animals, insects, fungus and weather.

"Growing in BC is different than growing around Toronto, aye. The weather here on the Lower Mainland is mild in the summer, with occasional rain showers. The heavy rains start in September. If your crop isn't out of the ground by the middle of September, the buds get wet and moldy, usually gray mold (*botrytis*), sometimes powdery mildew starts earlier on leaves. Toronto is in the middle of the continent and a lot hotter and more humid. Plants grow faster, but still need to be out of the ground before the frost," said Vansterdan, with a strong Canadian accent.

If the weather cooperates and Vansterdan plants early in the year,

To plant in marshy, grassy areas, this grower cuts a square yard of moist sod from the ground with a shovel, turns the entire piece over (180 degrees) and plants in it.

clones establish a dense root system and don't need much water during the growing season. A heavy layer of mulch helps conserve water and combat weeds.

Hardening-off Cuttings and Seedlings

After clones have rooted in rockwool cubes for three weeks, Vansterdan transplants them into 4-inch pots full of organic soil mix. He handles root cubes carefully and waters transplants heavily so roots grow into the new soil. He leaves the cuttings under a 400-watt HP sodium lamp for two weeks before moving them outdoors to harden-off in the greenhouse. He keeps clones in trays (nursery flats) so they are easy to handle. Since there is not enough room for all of the transplanted clones in the greenhouse, Vansterdan fills the greenhouse three different times. The first crop of clones is transplanted into the soil or 3-gallon pots and set out in the back yard garden after they have hardened-off for two or three weeks. The second crop of clones is moved in to harden-off and later transplanted to the local mountain plots. The third set of clones is moved into the greenhouse and grown until they are about 18 inches tall before he prompts flowering. Vansterdan covers the greenhouse to induce flowering with 12 hours of darkness.

Transplanting to the Mountain Site

The clones he transplants to the mountain site are grown in a tall container to promote a strong deep root system. The containers Vansterdan uses to clone the plants in are 6 inches tall and 3 inches square.

"I learned this trick when I worked for the Forest Service, aye," explained Vansterdan, "They grow tree seedlings in tall containers so they will have a deep strong root system. The deep, dense root system makes a strong plant, aye. I won't be able to water or give much care to these babies. A strong root system makes up for the lack of care".

"I try to go back and check on the clones two or three times after I plant them. Every time I go back there I pee around the plants to scare the deer and rabbits away. I also save urine in a bottle and sprinkle it around them, because I run out," said Vansterdan with a grin.

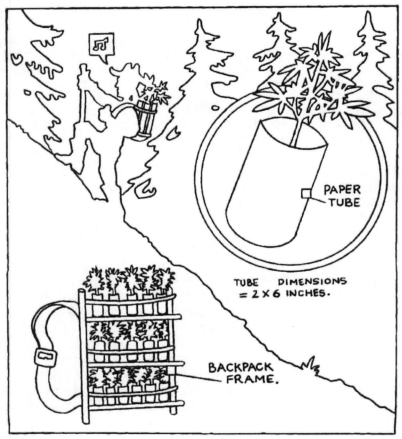

Clones in tall containers with a deep root system have the best chance of survival in remote, low maintenance gardens.

Seed Germination and Care

Cannabis seeds need only water, heat and air to germinate. Seeds, without light, properly watered, will germinate in 2 – 10 days, in temperatures from 70 – 90 degrees F. Germination is faster at higher temperatures but declines if temperatures climb above 90 degrees F. When the seed germinates, the outside protective shell splits and a tiny, white sprout (tap root) pops out. The seed leaves emerge from within the shell as they push upward in search of light.

Other Growers transplant foot-tall clones with smaller root systems. They remove the first few sets of leaves and bury the root ball deeper in the ground, leaving only six inches of foliage above ground. The clone will grow roots along the underground stem in the next few weeks.

One popular way to germinate seeds is placing seeds in a moist paper towel or cheesecloth, in a warm room, (70 – 90 degrees F.) and make sure they are in darkness.

Water the cloth daily, keep it moist and let excess water drain away freely. The seed germinates in a few days. The seed contains an adequate food supply for germination and watering with a mild mix of liquid fertilizer will hasten growth. In humid climates, water with a mild bleach or fungicide solution (2 - 5 drops per gallon) to prevent fungus. Plant seeds once the white sprout is visible. Do not expose the tender rootlet to prolonged, intense light or wind. Plant the germinated seed ¼" to ½ " deep in planting medium with the white sprout tip (the root) pointing down. Lay the seed on its side if confused about which end is up.

The second popular germination method is to sow the seed in a shallow planter (flat), peat pellet or rooting cube and keep the planting medium evenly moist. Transplant 2 – 4 weeks after the seedling emerges from the soil. Use a spoon to remove the root ball and keep it intact when transplanting.

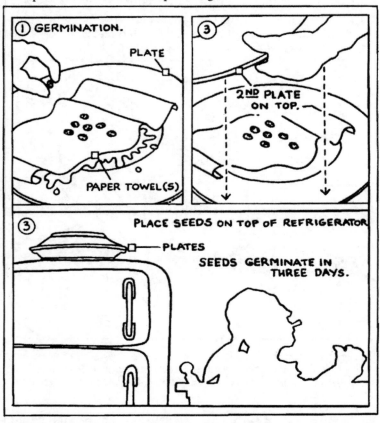

Germinating seeds between moist paper towels virtually ensures success.

A heat pad or heat tape under or in soil will accelerate germination without drying the soil too fast. A common problem for novices when germinating seeds is over-watering. Keep the soil uniformly moist, but not soggy. Plant seeds in a nursery flat and put them in a warm (not hot) place like on top of the refrigerator. Put a wet piece of paper on top of the soil to retain the moisture. Remove the paper as soon as seeds sprout through soil. Leaving the paper on the soil will inhibit growth. Often seeds only need one initial watering when this method is used. A shallow flat or planter with a heat pad underneath may require daily watering, while a deep, one gallon pot needs water every 2 or 3 days. When the surface is dry (¼-inch deep) it is time to water. Remember, there are few roots to absorb the water early in life and they are very delicate.

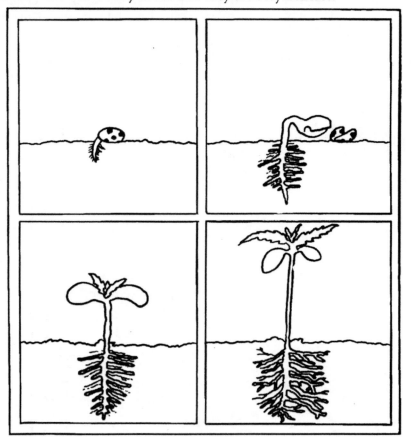

At germination, a seed sprouts, sets roots, grows roundish cotyledon leaves and the first set of true leaves.

Seedling (cotyledon) leaves are the first to appear after the seed sprouts above the soil. Within a few days, the first true leaves will grow. During the seedling stage, a root system grows rapidly and green growth is slow. The new root system is very small and requires a modest but constant supply of water. Too much water drowns roots, causing root rot or damping-off. Lack of water dries the infant root system. As the seedlings mature, some will grow faster and stronger. Others will be weak and leggy. Vansterdan thins out weak plants the third to fifth week and transplants seedlings without any damage.

Soil Temperature

Root cubes, made from rockwool, peat or Oasis™, are convenient and encourage a strong root system. Peat pots are small compressed peat moss containers with an outside permeable wall. The flat pellets pop-up into a seedling pot when watered. Place the seed or cutting in the wet root cube and keep it evenly moist. For clones, make sure to crimp the top in around the stem so firm contact is made between the stem and the growing medium. When roots show through the sides of the cube it is time to transplant. Slit the side and remove the expandable nylon shell of peat pots before transplanting. When completed properly seedlings and clones suffer no transplant shock. Check peat pots or root cubes daily. Keep them evenly moist, but not soggy. Root cubes and peat pots contain no nutrients. Feed seedlings after the first week and clones as soon as they are rooted with ¼ to ½ strength fertilizer.

Inexpensive heat cables double root growth and are easy to use.

The seed intensive method:

Planting many seeds in a small area is also an option. In loose fertile soil, plant seeds from ¼ to ½- inch deep. Some growers set up small 3 x 3 square foot sites, planting three rows with a seed every few inches. Growers with 4 or 5 small patches are virtually guaranteed a harvest. They grow 2 to 5 small plants in various sites. Infrared photography is less effective against small patches. To make more space, growers cull out weak plants at 4 – 5 weeks and remove males as they appear.

Cloning

Unlike humans, *cannabis* can be reproduced both sexually and asexually. Seeds are the product of sexual propagation; clones are the outcome of asexual or vegetative propagation. What *cannabis* growers call cloning is cutting a branch tip and rooting it. Technically cloning is reproducing plants from a single cell.

Once the sex of a plant is known and it is a female at least two months old, it's time to clone.

Clones yield an exact genetic replica of the mother plant. A female plant will reproduce females exactly like the mother. Occasionally, a male flower will appear on a clone of a known female, or a plant will have mutated or different growth than other clones from the same plant.

Clones from the same plant grow into identical adults if grown in the exact same environment. The same clones grown in different climates may look like different plants.

Cloning also has some negative points. The mother plant will produce clones just like her, if she is not perfect or disease resistant, clones also share this weakness.

Cloning is simple and easy. A 100 percent survival rate can be achieved by following the simple procedures outlined below.

Most clones taken in the vegetative stage tend to root quickly and grow fast. Clones taken from flowering plants may root quickly but require more than a month to revert back to vegetative growth and they might flower prematurely.

Cloning changes a plant's chemistry. The stem that once grew leaves, must now grow roots in order to survive. All sprays should be avoided now as they compound cloning stress.

Clones root faster when stems have a high carbohydrate and low nitrogen concentration. Flushing soil with water leaches out nutrients, including nitrogen. Leaves can also be leached directly by reverse foliar feeding. Use clean, tepid water to mist foliage heavily, daily, for a week, to wash nitrogen out of foliage rapidly. Carbohydrate content is usually highest in lower, older mature branches. A rigid branch that will fold over quickly forming a 90-degree angle when bent, rather than bend, is a good sign of high carbohydrate content. While rooting, clones require a minimum of nitrogen and increased levels of phosphorus to promote root growth.

Root growth stimulants are available in liquid, gel or powder forms. Professionals prefer the liquid or gel rooting hormones for penetration and consistency. They avoid powder types because they adhere inconsistently to the stem and yield a lower survival rate.

NOTE: Some of these products are not recommended for use with edible plants, so read the label carefully before deciding to use a product.

Clones root faster when the soil is warm, 70 – 80 degrees F. The clones will transpire less if the air is about 5 degrees F. cooler than the soil. Misting clones with water is a good way to cool foliage and lower transpiration.

"Every time I start cloning a new variety, I try 5 - 10 practice clones before making a serious cloning," said Vansterdan, knife in hand.

The sex of plants can be determined by growing them until they're four inches high, then decreasing the amount of light they receive to eight hours. Cull males when they show sex in one or two weeks.

Several growers I interviewed reported that giving female plants two days of complete darkness will make them produce male flowers.

Plant Sex

Growers can sometimes tell plant sex about the 12th week of growth, that's when male and female plants begin to differentiate. Males often grow a single white spur from a sheath at each branch node (at the base of the stem). Females sometimes grow two long white pre-flower pistils from a similar sheath. The presence of one spur or two white pistils does not necessarily designate sex in plants grown from seed. The only way to tell for sure is when actual flowers appear when plants experience shorter days. See color photographs.

Starting in mid August, Vansterdan inspects plants carefully every day and removes the males when they show flowers. He then unceremoniously dries the boys out and smokes the raspy leaves or gives foliage away to friends.

Clones are available all year round. Last year, Vansterdan wanted to know the sex of plants he grew from seed before he put them out in the back yard. The seeds were so expensive he did not want to put all his energy into growing females. He grew them from seed and practiced cloning for sex.

Cloning for Sex

Distinguish male and female plants 100 percent of the time and not alter the parent plants growth cycle by cloning for sex.

To clone for sex, take two cuttings (one could die) from each parent plant in question. Label each clone and corresponding parent.

When rooting, give clones only 12 hours of light. Set clones in a totally dark closet or place a box over them. The 12 hour photoperiod will induce flowering. The clone will show its sex within two weeks. Harvest all males, except those used for breeding and keep females. Males may also be cloned and induced to flower when pollen is needed for breeding. Use the sexed clones to eliminate male parent plants you don't need, keeping females to provide future clones.

Leave the parent plants outdoors in the summer sun to maintain vegetative growth. Give the clones 12 hours of light by covering them with a cardboard box or place them somewhere in total darkness. Make sure the clones get 12 hours of light and 12 hours of uninterrupted, total darkness every 24 hours. If light leaks or you forget to cover the plants, flower induction takes longer. Once you have harvested the sexed females clones, you can decide which mothers you like best.

Cloning: Step-by-Step

Step One: Choose a mother plant that is at least two months old and 24 inches tall. Leach the soil daily with at least two gallons of water per 4 gallons of soil, (make sure drainage is good) or wash down leaves (reverse foliar feeding) heavily every morning. Start one week before taking cuttings and leach every morning. This will wash out the nitrogen.

Step Two: Choose older lower branch tips to clone. With a sharp blade, make a 45 degree cut across firm, healthy 1/8- to ¼-inch-wide branches, 2 to 8 inches in length. Don't smash the end of the stem when making the cut. Trim off two or three sets of leaves. There should be at least two sets of leaves above the soil line and one or two sets of trimmed nodes below the ground. Make the cut halfway between the sets of nodes. Immediately place the cut end in fresh, tepid water.

Step Three: Use peat pots or root cubes to facilitate maintenance and transplanting. Fill small containers or nursery flats with coarse, washed sand, fine vermiculite, soilless mix or if nothing else is available, use fine potting soil. Saturate with tepid water. Use a pencil or chopstick to make a hole in the rooting medium a little larger than the stem. The bottom of the hole should be at least one half inch from the bottom of the container.

Step Four: Use a root hormone for softwood cuttings. Most

Vansterdan takes clones from mother plants in the greenhouse. He dips the clone in rooting hormone before sticking it in a rockwool cube. In three weeks the clones are well rooted and ready for transplanting outdoors.

growers prefer a liquid or gel. Mix it just before using. Swirl each cutting in the hormone gel/liquid solution for 10 - 20 seconds or roll stem in powder hormone. Place the cuttings in the hole. Pack rooting medium gently around the stem.

Step Five: Lightly water with a mild solution of vitamin B[1] until the surface is evenly moist. Water as needed.

Step Six: Clones root best with 18 to 24 hours of fluorescent light. Use 12 hours of light if cloning to determine sex.

Step Seven: Place a tent over rooting clones to keep humidity near 80 percent. Construct the tent out of baggies, plastic film or glass. Remember to leave a breezeway so the little clones can breathe. An alternative is to mist the rooting clones with tepid water several times daily. Either method helps to retain moisture, since there are no roots to supply the leaves with water.

Step Eight: The humidity tent will maintain the temperature at about 70 – 80 degrees F.

Step Nine: Some cuttings may wilt for a few days or the leaves may rot if touching moist soil. Remove rotten leaves. Clones should look normal by the end of the week.

Step Ten: Clones root in one to four weeks, leaf tips turn yellow, and roots grow out the bottom root cubes; clones start vertical growth. To check for root growth in flats or pots, carefully remove a clone to see if it has good root development.

Transplanting Small Seedlings:
Growers that transplant small seedlings find that survival rate increases greatly when compared to moving large plants. Mobility and security are main concerns when moving seedlings. Successful growers grow seedlings in easy-to-transport containers with a deep space for roots and acclimate (harden-off) plants to their new outdoor environment before transplanting.

Transplanting
When plants have outgrown their container, transplant into a larger pot to ensure roots room for sustained rapid growth. Inhibiting the root system stunts plants. Some of the signs are slow, sickly growth and leggy, spindly plants. Transplant into the same type of soil. Vansterdan starts seeds and clones in small root cubes or peat pots which are very easy to transplant.

"Smaller root cubes are easier to transplant and mix with the soil better. I used 3 and 4-inch rockwool cubes at first but they stayed too wet and the roots penetrated the soil slowly, aye. The small cubes dry out faster so roots penetrate the soil faster," said Vansterdan.

Transplanting is traumatic. Minute root hairs are super delicate and easily destroyed by light, air or clumsy hands. Roots grow in darkness, where their environment is rigid and secure. Roots taken out of contact with soil dry out and die quickly. Be careful!

Disturb the root system as little as possible when transplanting. Vitamin B[1] helps ease transplant shock. Plants need time to settle-in and re-establish their normal constant supply of fluids from the roots through the plant. They require low levels of nitrogen and potassium and large quantities of phosphorus. When Vitamin B[1] is applied properly and roots are disturbed little, there is no sign of transplant shock or wilt.

"I transplant late in the day so plants have all night to recover. I water heavily after transplanting to pack the soil around roots so they are in constant contact with soil and don't dry out. Then I give transplants less intense light for a couple of days to further ease transplant shock," said Vansterdan.

Healthy plants suffer less transplant shock. Nonetheless, transplanting a sick, root bound plant to a large container or into a planting hole has cured more than one ailing plant.

Transplanting Step-by-Step

This example shows how Vansterdan transplants a one month old seedling started in a root cube into the outdoor garden.

Step One: Harden-off seedlings by placing them outdoors a few hours daily so they acclimate to the harsher climate. Bring tender seedlings in at night. Leave them out more hours each day. By the end of a week they should harden-off.

Step Two: Water seedling with ½-strength Vitamin B^1, one or two days before transplanting.

Step Three: Prepare planting hole: See Chapter Three

Step Four: Water soil until saturated.

Step Five: Carefully remove rooted seedling along with individual root cube. If in soil be careful to keep the root ball in one integral piece.

Step Six: Carefully place root cube in a prepared hole in the outdoor garden. Make sure all roots are growing down.

Step Seven: Backfill around the root ball. Gently, but firmly place soil into contact with root ball.

Step Eight: Water with ½ strength Vitamin B^1, until the soil is

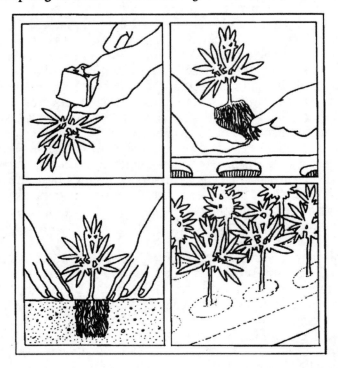

To transplant, carefully remove the root ball from container, lightly separate roots if compacted, place in pre-made hole, backfill and water heavily.

completely saturated, but not soggy.

Step Nine: Place new transplants under a screen or in the shade to subdue light for a couple of days. Gradually move to full sun in 3 – 4 days.

Step Ten: Rich, fertile, organic soil will supply enough nutrients for about a month or longer before supplemental fertilization is necessary.

Growing the Crop

The weather had warmed by the late spring and the freestanding greenhouse did not need to be heated any longer. Vansterdan removed the plants and the Styrofoam floor from the greenhouse. Once empty, he removed the greenhouse and cultivated the rich, organic soil below to get it ready for planting. Next he moved in the last crop of clones, transplanting them into the bed he had prepared with soil amendments (see Appendix) the fall before. He set the greenhouse on six-inch blocks over the clones. The gap below allows extra ventilation. On hot days, Vansterdan opens the top of the greenhouse so air can flow from below and out the ceiling.

The clones were established in the rich soil in a few days and began to grow. In about a month the small clones had grown about 18 inches tall. That's when he started foliar feeding with a super bloom formula every three or four days. He also started covering the greenhouse every day with a dark blanket so plants would receive 12 hours of light and a full 12 hours of darkness to induce flowering.

"Ventilation is the main problem when it's hot and I'm flowering a crop in the little greenhouse. I keep it covered all morning, when the weather is cool. I take the cover off mid to late morning. I keep the top open so it gets plenty of ventilation and it still gets 12 hours of light," said Vansterdan as he looked up the sunrise and sunset schedule in the newspaper and continued, "you know it gets light a half hour before sunrise and stays light a half hour after sunset."

The backyard clones grew so big they had to be bent and pruned back so they didn't shade the vegetables. Vansterdan gave them little care other than regular watering. In mid August, he tilled in bat guano so they would set larger flowers.

The mountain clones received no care.

Harvest

The small greenhouse was the easiest of all to harvest. The clones were ripe 8 to 9 weeks after he initiated flowering. Vansterdan cut plants off at the base, removed large leaves and hung them on a line in the drying room. See Chapter Four for more information.

Vansterdan harvested buds in the backyard garden, one bud at a time. Buds that received more light matured sooner than shaded buds. To harvest, he removed the large leaves around the buds, including leaf stem (petiole), while the plant was still growing. Next he snipped off each bud-laden branch with pruners, setting them in a cardboard box. When the box was full, he brought the buds inside to the drying room.

Plants in the mountain garden became ripe at different times and harvest required three separate trips to the garden patches. He harvested complete plants in the mountain garden by cutting them off at the base without removing any large fan leaves. He cut branches in 2- to 3-foot pieces so they would fit into his backpack. He removed large stems, cut them into small pieces and scattered them in the area to decompose.

"I got lucky this year, the rain came late and we had no trouble with powdery mildew or bud mold. I think I'll celebrate and have a smoke, I do have a selection, aye," said Vansterdan staring at 80 pounds of drying marijuana.

See Harvest, Chapter Four.

Setting the greenhouse up on blocks and opening the top a few inches should provide enough ventilation for most days. If the days get exceptionally warm, raise the greenhouse up higher and remove the top.

Warm, Arid Coastal Climate
California, Spain, Italy

Introduction

Conchita lives near the Mediterranean Sea in Spain where the climate is warm and mild most of the year. The sun shines hot and bright on many of those mild days, baking the rocky clay soil. This soil drains poorly and is difficult for roots to penetrate.

Like her mother and grandmother, Conchita grows *cannabis*. Two years ago, Conchita teamed up with another grower, Felipe, who fled the repressive *cannabis* laws in the United States and relocated in Spain. The climate in Spain is very similar to the climate in California where Felipe grew marijuana for more than twenty years. Felipe was able to transfer his growing knowledge to Spain and cultivate superb crops with Conchita.

Conchita and Felipe have three separate gardens. One is close to the Mediterranean Sea where they live, another is a few miles inland and the third garden is in the mountains. The gardens in the coastal city are located on the flat roof of their apartment building and their sunny balcony. The inland garden is planted in the abandoned barn courtyard at Conchita's grand parents' farm. The mountain garden is a days travel away and requires little care. They also have a small indoor grow room illuminated by a 250-watt High Pressure sodium lamp and two fluorescent tubes.

Site Selection

"After kick-ass seeds, a grow site needs good soil, a water supply, at least 6 hours of direct midday sun and it's gotta be secure," said Felipe with the authority of a seasoned American guerilla grower.

"California used to be great, you could hide a few plants in your back yard or in the hills. Now growers are climbing 50 – 80 feet up trees in Northern California and planting on stands in the canopy to avoid detection! The paranoia is so thick during harvest season that you can cut it up and roll it in a joint. I've had it with the heavy-handed armed commando-type DEA agents, cops and opportunistic marijuana thieves in the America. That's why I moved, I couldn't take it any more. Here I can harvest my crop and not be persecuted," said Felipe emotionally.

Felipe made a pilgrimage to several seed companies in Amsterdam, and bought seed packets of 'Neville's Haze', 'Super Silver Haze', 'El Nino', 'White Rhino', 'White Widow' and 'Great White Shark', 'Jack Herer', 'Jack Flash', and 'Shiva Shanti'. The long growing season is perfect for the predominately sativa 'Haze' varieties and the other seeds grow well outdoors.

The sun is at a higher angle during the summer months and brighter. More sun shines on the south side of any plant or structure. Southeast orientation receives morning sun and if facing the southwest, plants get evening sun.

Laws in the USA provide for forfeiture of assets that are proceeds of, or have been used to commit the "crime" of cultivating *cannabis*. Gardeners that plant marijuana on their own turf often forfeit their land and all their assets if arrested. Authorities regularly take any assets they can sell. The proceeds from the sale of these assets often go directly to the law enforcement agency that made the arrest. If the gardener has children living at home, the state takes them too, normally at the time of arrest. Check your local laws! Growers living in a country with repressive laws often garden on public land or any property but their own. If the land owner knows that marijuana is growing on the property, they could forfeit their land and be prosecuted along with the grower!

Spain and Portugal occupy the Iberian Peninsula in Western Europe where the sun shines virtually year round. It's a grower's paradise. The eastern and southern coasts enjoy the mild influence of the Mediterranean Sea. Some natural inland microclimates keep temperatures warm enough to cultivate marijuana 6 to 12 months of the year. The northern coast is influenced by the chilling Atlantic Ocean; it has more rainfall and cooler temperatures. The lush green landscape is similar to that of Northern Europe, Northwest America/ southwestern Canada or Tazmania. Spain has almost as many different growing climates as North America.

Site selection was very easy for Conchita and Felipe. Their balcony garden is on the 5th floor and difficult to see from the street. During 7 – 8 months of the year, the balcony receives 5 – 6 hours of sunlight daily. The rooftop terrace is secure and sunny all day. Conchita's aunt and uncle own a rustic farm about 24 miles (40 kilometers) inland from the coast. The soil is clay and compacted, with a pH of about 8. Most of the 30-foot-square (10-meter-square) courtyard receives full sun all day long. The gate of the barn's courtyard is locked and tall walls on all four sides hide the interior from public view. Conchita's aunt and uncle live on the property and do not use the barn area. They are delighted that Conchita and Felipe are using it to grow marijuana. Felipe found the remote mountain garden (elevation 2,600 feet, 850 meters) patch, located on public land, last spring while hunting wild mushrooms. Sunshine is abundant during the seven-month growing season. The soil is rocky, full of minerals and little else.

Felipe brought *The Western Garden Book* (Sunset Publishing Co., Menlo Park, CA, USA) with him from America. This book is a wealth of information about the specific microclimates in Western North America.

The gardening renaissance fueled by the baby boom generation in North America has spawned many new regional gardening books and flower/vegetable seed catalogs. These publications are packed with right-on information about growing in specific microclimates. Smart guerilla growers apply the information provided by these books and catalogs to grow marijuana in their microclimates.

Smart growers make friends with local nursery people and gardeners and find out how and when they plant and grow tomatoes and other vegetables to get the best yield. They read the garden column in local newspapers and magazines. Insect and fungus infestations are usually monitored by local garden columnists. Learning about problems before they happen makes averting them easier.

Rogue Pollen from Hemp and Misplaced Males

Industrial hemp and rogue male pollen can drift from a few feet to hundreds of miles to settle and pollinate flowering females. In cities, rogue male pollen creates troubles for rooftop, balcony and backyard gardeners. Negligent neighbors often fail to spot or remove flowering male plants. A slight breeze on a hot dry sunny day can carry this pollen across the city to sinsemilla crops. Depending on the mass of pollen, tops can be partially to fully pollinated.

Both rural and urban guerilla growers face the specter of transient hemp pollen from commercial hemp fields. Crops could be unknowingly fertilized. Industrial fiber hemp *cannabis* is grown legally in Western and Eastern Europe, Canada, Australia and many other countries. Growers check with local farmers and the ministry of agriculture to find out where commercial hemp crops are grown. They also study local wind and weather patterns to figure out where the pollen will drift. Moisture, rain and high humidity are airborne pollens' foremost enemies. Pollen originating in the low-quality Moroccan hash fields often drifts north to Spain. During dry weather conditions, a large percentage of the pollen is viable upon arrival. Each percent humidity increases, more pollen is rendered inviable.

Once pollinated, female plants turn energy into producing seed. New resin and flower production slows to a crawl. If high THC content plants are fertilized by low THC content marijuana or industrial hemp, offsprings often look great and smell good, but will not get you high.

Growers with rogue pollen as a problem can grow cuttings indoors and transplant outdoors later in the year so females start to flower after industrial hemp, which flowers from mid August to September, and unchecked male plants have released most or all of their pollen. They also plant in wind shadows, large divots on south-facing hillsides, areas where winds seldom travel.

If the problem is severe, growers plant a spring crop in a greenhouse and induce flowering with 12 hours of darkness. Other growers plant in a greenhouse and keep a vent fan blowing. Intake air comes in through an opening covered by a moist towel. One edge of the towel rests in a bucket of water to wick moisture. They also wet down the greenhouse exterior to kill any wild borne pollen.

Smart growers call the local air quality agency and ask for a recent air quality analysis, including hemp pollen. They explain that they are allergic to hemp pollen, and need to know everything they can about it.

Security

Spanish police do not aggressively look for marijuana gardens and gardeners. They don't fly around looking for marijuana with infrared sensors and other high-tech spy toys developed for war. Security is a matter of keeping the garden behind a wall, on a protected balcony or in a remote, inaccessible, rural location. A few unlucky growers have overbearing neighbors that demand police pay marijuana growers a visit. Normally the police pull the plants and leave.

Growers take simple security measures such as registering their house or apartment in the name of another person and not bragging (too much) about their crop. Growers who live under the siege of the marijuana inquisition can not tell anybody about their hobby. Not even family members can be trusted. Gardeners are forced to lie to their friends and family about their plant preference. Many growers lead a double life, with two sets of friends, those that don't know and the trusted few who do. Any time the subject comes up, the easiest route for a persecuted gardener is to conform to hard-line "drug" policy and refer to marijuana growers as criminals that are a burden on society. Often these growers paint a picture that eliminates them from suspicion.

Site Preparation and Planting

The Barnyard Garden

Felipe performed the simple soil test outlined in "What Kind of Soil Do You Have?" The test results showed that the rocky soil is held together with heavy clay that drains poorly. This soil is hard as hell when dry. The tests did not show the mineral content of the soil. Spanish soil, depending on location, has high concentrations of sodium, calcium, iron and magnesium, which affects the pH and uptake of nutrients. Sodium causes the worst problems. The gardeners decided that it would be easier to blend their own soil rather than trying to work with existing dirt.

Felipe and Conchita also read the sections in the Appendix on pH, water, soil, compost and fertilizers before preparing their growing sites.

Years of experience taught Felipe to prepare the soil for grow sites at least a month before planting. "I like to add lots of compost and manure to the soil. The earth here is mostly clay, so adding organic matter improves drainage and water-holding ability. I can't always find aged manure that will not burn tender transplants. I mix compost with fresh manure and let it age a month or more so it cools down and doesn't burn plants," explained Felipe. He continued, "I stay away from manure with a high salt content. They usually give beef cattle extra salt (sodium nitrate) so they gain weight faster. This salt comes out in their urine and manure. A little salt is OK, too much salt locks up nutrients and stunts plants".

The barnyard soil was compacted after 25 years of laying bare and fallow. It also lacked available nutrients. Conchita had long been friends with a neighbor named Gregorio, who kept a small dairy herd. Gregorio cleaned out his milking barn regularly. He had been removing the manure/straw from the barn for years and piling it up near the barn. Gregorio gave them five loads, three cubic yards apiece (15 total) of the well-rotted manure/straw compost mix.

They had two choices to prepare the soil: dig individual holes for each plant, or lightly till the surface, add compost/manure and make raised beds. They decided to dig large planting holes for each plant and fill each one with their own rich compost/manure soil mix.

Digging a large, deep hole and filling it with perfect soil is an ideal way to improve poor soil quickly. The bigger the hole the better. The rationale is simple; roots grow deeply into the ground in search of water and nutrients. In perfect soil 3 – 4 feet deep, water is retained evenly, deep, strong roots grow stronger, healthier plants that are easier to maintain. Growers that invest a little extra work in the beginning are paid back many times over. They have few problems and harvest thick, resin-packed buds.

"We used a jackhammer to break up the rocky clay. We borrowed an electric jackhammer and portable generator from a plumber friend of ours, plugged it in and started breaking up the hardpan. The jackhammer saved us hours of work," said Felipe with a satisfied smile.

After a well-timed heavy rain, the hard clay soil was ready to work. Felipe and Conchita used the jackhammer, picks and shovels to make the planting holes in the barnyard. They decided to experiment with the sizes and shapes of holes. They dug some of the holes 3 x 3 x 3-feet-square (1 x 1 x 1 yard square), others they made 2 yards across, 8 inches deep and sloped down to the 1-yard bottom. A sloped hole follows the natural contour of the roots and allows easy penetration. They used the jackhammer to loosen the soil in the bottom of the 3-foot-deep holes another foot deeper without removing the soil. They piled the soil next to each hole, taking care to separate the thin layer of topsoil from other layers of rocky subsoil. The heavy clay soil formed an underground container for their soil mix. Water penetrates the rocky clay soil slowly and stays inside the hole.

After two days of hard work with a jackhammer, picks and shovels, Conchita and Felipe had dug 20 holes that measured about one cubic yard each.

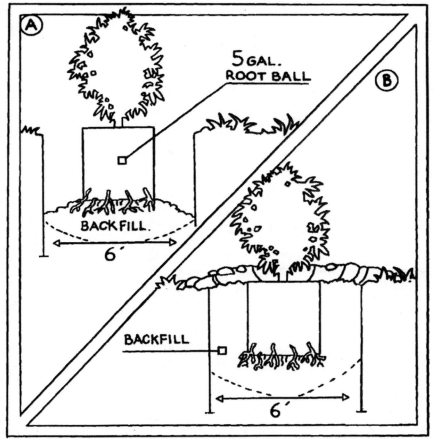

Digging a large planting hole and filling it with a fertile soil mix increases yield up to tenfold.

They backfilled each of the holes in layers. First they threw in a 4-inch layer of small rocks and mixed steamed bone meal with soil to form another 8-inch layer. They filled the balance with a thin layer of topsoil with the rich compost/manure/straw, rock phosphate and seaweed meal. They mounded the compost/soil mix up about a foot above ground level so it could settle during the growing season. See "Organic Fertilizer" in the Appendix.

Next, they piled up left over subsoil to form a bowl around each hole that helps catch rainwater.

"I thought Felipe was crazy when he said we had to dig those holes. I was sure he was a sado-masochist and was trying to make me one too. I hated it! But he showed me photos of his two-kilo (dried manicured buds) plants in California. From now on, I'll always

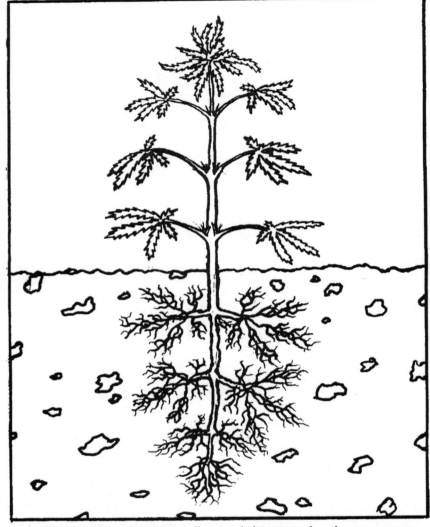

Roots penetrate the soil and normally grow below ground at the same rate as the plant grows above ground.

plant in big holes," said Conchita.

Once the holes were prepared and watered heavily, it was time to take 70 clones from mother plants growing indoors. Six weeks after taking clones, they would be ready to transplant outdoors. See "Cloning" Chapter Two. Digging 20 holes was hard work, planting clones made the most sense. If they planted seedlings, some would grow male plants and they would not have mother plants to make more clones.

To grow seedlings and clones, Felipe hung a 250-watt HP sodium lamp on an adjustable chain in the corner of a room. He germinated seedlings in a shallow flat of commercial potting soil. The soil supplied enough nutrients for the first month of growth. When seeds sprouted he transplanted them into three-liter containers full of commercial potting soil. He packed the pots next to one another and moved the HP sodium 18 inches above. He kept the room temperature between 65 and 80 degrees F. with the help of a extraction fan. Felipe was careful to keep the soil evenly moist and not overwater. He used *only* distilled water to irrigate seedlings, mother plants and clones. Tap water and bottled mineral water have too many dissolved solids and cause nutrient uptake problems.

Felipe fertilized only once with ½-strength liquid fertilizer two weeks before transplanting.

The clones rooted for three weeks under fluorescent light and grew another three weeks under the 250-watt HP sodium lamp. They kept both the fluorescent and the HP sodium on 24 hours a day. The light regimen promoted a little more growth and saved them the expense of buying a timer. The 6-week-old clones were bushy, strong and healthy.

They culled out the 10 weakest clones and retained 60 clones in 4-inch pots. Every day Conchita moved the clones outdoors for a few hours of direct sunlight and back indoors during the cool nights. (See Hardening-off and Transplanting Chapter Two).

Most of the gardeners in this climate plant tomatoes in April. Tomatoes and marijuana share many of the same climatic needs. Planting marijuana clones and seedlings when experienced locals plant tomatoes is smart gardening.

Balcony and Terrace Gardens

Conchita and Felipe love seafood and frequent the local fish market. Conchita had a brainstorm while sucking the butter out of a prawn body: "Let's grow in the white Styrofoam boxes they pack fish in. They make perfect pots for hot balconies and terraces!"

The lightweight low profile containers measure 18-inch-square and 12 inches deep. The white Styrofoam insulates the root zone from the sweltering heat. Mark, the clerk, gave them 15 Styrofoam containers.

Felipe cut six ½-inch holes in the bottom of each Styrofoam container and cleaned them with soap and water. Next, he lined each container with several sheets of newspaper before filling with potting soil they bought at the local nursery. Newspaper helps retain water and keeps soil from falling out the drainage holes.

"The last few years, I used dirt from the back yard, packed it into clay pots and grew plants on the balcony. That soil didn't hold water evenly and the clay pots got hot as hell. I didn't realize it at the time, but the roots cooked in the hot pots. By changing to store-bought soil and white insulated pots, our harvest doubled!" said Conchita with a twinkle in her eye. She continued, "I love white Styrofoam. Before I met Felipe, I didn't have a clue how water penetrates soil. Hot soil dries and forms a crevice alongside the container, transforming it into a 'dead root zone'. Trying to grow roots in a 'dead root zone' is like trying to grow ferns on the Sahara Desert!"

> If gophers, moles, rabbits, etc. are a problem, line holes with 1-inch mesh chicken wire one foot deep before transplanting. Exclude animals and birds from tender seedlings and clones with an inconspicuous wire or nylon fence. Once the plants get bigger and tougher they will be less appealing to animals and birds. If secrecy is an issue, camouflage the fence and surrounding area with local debris.

Potting soil from the garden center has better texture and is more fertile than all but the best backyard soils mixed with compost. The pH and the composition of most store-bought potting soils are listed on the side of the bag. Growers in high-rainfall areas mix a handful of dolomite lime (the finest flour grade) in each container to keep the pH stable and add magnesium and calcium to the mix.

After hardening-off 30 six-week old clones for a week, they planted two clones in each of the 15 containers.

The Mountain Garden

"It takes us 6 hours by car to get to the garden in the mountains. Every time we go there we travel two days and work one day. We only go there twice a year, about the first of May, after the rains stop. We return in late September to harvest. The garden has to take care of itself," said Felipe more businesslike than I have ever seen him.

To prepare the soil on the sunny, southern hillside, they cleared the weeds and dug a small terrace for each hole in between the large rocks, brush and low-growing trees. They dug 20 holes about 18-inch-square and piled up the extra rocks around the perimeter. They backfilled the holes with a mix of peat moss, soil, polymer crystals and slow-acting layers of organic fertilizer.

Placing a piece of wood or plastic in the bottom of the hole makes water puddle up at the bottom and slows drainage. They could have also placed polymer crystals,* gravel, vermiculite or anything that would help retain water in the bottom of the hole.

*polymer crystals are small crystals that expand to about 15 times their size when moistened by water. They are added to soil to

A small low-profile greenhouse is inconspicuous on a rooftop balcony.

extend the time between watering.

They planted two female clones in each hole and irrigated with rainwater siphoned from barrels they had in their vehicle. After watering heavily, they collected debris from around the area and mulched around the plants to help retain water and slow weed growth.

Water

Water in Spain is packed with dissolved solids, also called "mineral impurities" and "ionic salts," that affect both the pH and availability of nutrients (See Water and pH in Appendix). Often the pH is beyond the 5.8 to 7 range, which impairs the uptake of nutrients. Desert regions in the interior and along the Mediterranean have alkaline water with a pH above 7. High rainfall areas influenced

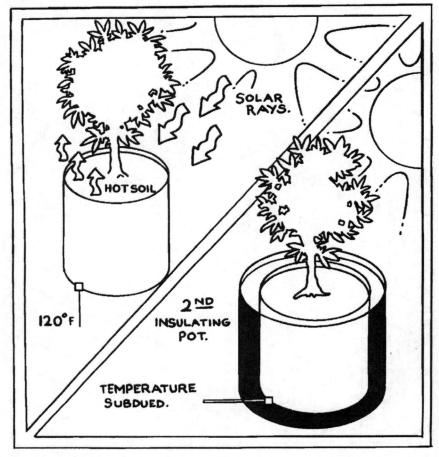

SOLAR RAYS.

HOT SOIL

120°F

2ND INSULATING POT.

TEMPERATURE SUBDUED.

A container in the hot sun cooks root at temperature of 120 degrees F or higher. Place one pot inside another pot to keep the root ball cool. Growers report this simple trick has doubled their harvest.

by the Atlantic Ocean are frequently acidic with a *p*H below 7. Excessive dissolved solids in irrigation water cause some nutrients to become unavailable. Excess salts inhibit seed germination, burn tender root hairs and tips or edges of leaves and stunt plants. Water is salty inland 20 miles or more from the sea. Salt builds up to toxic levels when soil is watered with salty (brackish) water if drainage is insufficient. That water is packed with dissolved solids is a fact too often overlooked by growers.

Felipe used a dissolved solids (DS) meter to test the water at each of their three grow locations. He found the city water and the water at the country farm to have a DS concentration of more than

Always dig a planting hole that is as big as possible, especially if plants receive little or no maintenance.

250 PPM.

"I flipped when I saw the DS meter register 250 PPM! I had no idea the water was this loaded with salt. I thought the meter was broken, so I took the readings again and again; the results were the same. The meter registers only the total concentration of dissolved solids. I knew finding which salts were in the water was the first step to solving the problem," said Felipe with the look of a man who had just seen the salt specter.

Felipe knew that this water would stunt plants by at least half! That's right, half. A plant that should weigh two kilos would only weigh one kilo. Solving the water problem would double his production and not increase the work. There had to be a solution.

Felipe and Conchita talked to several local farmers and a Ministry of Agriculture man about the water. They learned that sodium causes big problems. Chlorides and sulfates are also troublemakers, but can be leached. Excess sodium in the water blocks other nutrients uptake. Marijuana can use only 5-10 PPM sodium, but more than 50 PPM are available. Once in solution, roots absorb sodium and don't absorb potassium, even if available. High concentrations of sodium draw nutrients and liquids out of roots.

Sodium has real staying power, too, and it's expensive to extract. Options include an expensive reverse osmosis machine ($1000 US). The machine passes salt tainted water through a membrane that lets only pure water through. Dissolved solids (ionic salts) are removed.

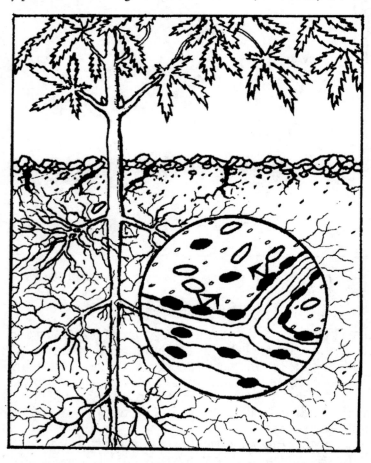

Nutrient uptake is blocked by sodium-rich water. Other important nutrients are unable to enter pass through the roots via osmosis. Wash excess sodium out of soil with clean water.

Deionization, passing water through two resins and replacing bad salts with innocuous hydroxyl and hydrogen is also expensive. Two other high-power options include distillation and electrodialysis.

Salty water tastes bad. The easiest and cheapest way for growers to detect dissolved solids is to check for residue when tainted water evaporates. The residue appears as a white film or dust where the water evaporated. Look for salt on the surface of the soil or around container drain holes. Clay pots often have whitish salt built up on the outside. If levels are low, few problems are caused with nutrient uptake. High levels, above 200 ppm, cause severe nutrient uptake problems. Clear signs of these problems might not appear for several weeks.

Rule of Thumb: Pour ½-liter of water into a large dark pan and let it evaporate. If a white film is visible, there are excessive dissolved solids in the water.

Highly soluble, sodium-packed water, accumulates quickly in the soil. Growers who water with sodium-rich water see plants grow slowly, with smaller leaves and shorter stature. Continued irrigation causes sodium stress, actually sucking the liquid out of roots and drying them out. The more sodium-rich water they are given the drier they get. Plants lose the ability to absorb water!

How much sodium is too much? If there is more than 50 ppm sodium, the grower must make amends from the start. Most water in Spain contains more than 50 PPM sodium.

Use only distilled water or rainwater to grow cuttings, seedlings and mother plants. Once plants are a month or two old, they are stronger and can withstand more sodium abuse. Monthly flushing is necessary. See below.

What to do with highly soluble, sodium laden water? One option for growers with 50 to 75 ppm sodium is to flush buildup out by "washing" the soil with three liters of water for every liter of soil. Leaching also flushes out excess chlorides and sulfates, a fair option for city growers that have lots of water and plants in pots.

"After transplanting, I water heavily with tap or well water that is packed with sodium. After that I add ammonium phosphate to the water which makes the sodium soluble and it washes out of the soil. The ammonium phosphate also adds nitrogen (ammonia) and phosphorous (phosphate) to the soil."

Growers with a limited water supply with more sodium in their water follow Felipe's advice to the letter.

Growers dissolve a small amount of ammonium phosphate in a barrel of irrigation water before watering plants.

Rainwater can also be mixed to dilute with the sodium-tainted water.

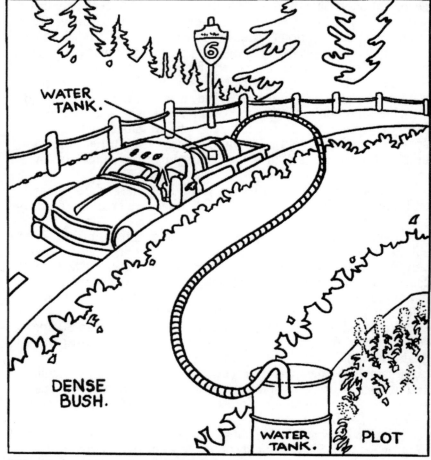

WATER TANK.

DENSE BUSH.

WATER TANK.

PLOT

This grower catches rainwater and gravity flows it to a reservoir.

To summarize, there are four cheap ways to improve water quality.

1. Water seedlings, clones and mother plants with distilled water or rainwater.

2. Flush container gardens with 3 liters of water for each liter of soil.

3. Mix 50 percent rainwater with tap water to dilute the dissolved salts.

4. Water once with tap water and always afterward with tap water containing ammonium sulfate.

Fertilizers

A limited selection of commercial fertilizers is available in Spain. Garden centers and farm supply stores carry a few chemical fertilizers in soluble, granular and time release form. Organic fertilizers come in the form of manures and other natural elements. See "Fertilizers" in Appendix.

Like the water, Spanish soil is packed with high levels of minerals. Sodium, calcium, and magnesium are again the big trouble makers. Solutions to excess sodium are found under "Water" above. Excess calcium keeps the *p*H too high and blocks uptake of several nutrients; iron is the most affected, followed by potassium. Make sure fertilizers contain chelated (available) iron to overcome this problem. See also Iron, Chlorosis and *p*H in Appendix. Excess magnesium creates rapid uptake of trace elements, but usually causes no problems.

Felipe and Conchita mixed organic fertilizers into the soil at the barnyard and mountain gardens to supply nutrients throughout the lifecycle and did not need to add any more fertilizers. If there were any problems: slow growth, burned leaf tips or leaf yellowing, they consulted the Fertilizer section in the Appendix for solutions.

They fertilized the plants on the balcony and rooftop terrace with a mild soluble flowering fertilizer for germination and seedling growth, when phosphorus intake is high. They changed to a high-nitrogen formula during vegetative growth and back to a "super

Clean rainwater is the absolute best for irrigation. Catching rainwater is easy, but be careful, roofs and terraces can accumulate trash that pollutes otherwise clean rainwater.

Please convert if necessary. The charts are in the Appendix. One millimeter of rainwater is one liter per square meter. To figure the possible amount of catchment rainwater, multiply the square meters of roof or terrace space by the annual rainfall. For example, a small terrace measures 5 meters by 6 meters is 30 square meters. (5 x 6 = 30). If annual rainfall is 100 millimeters (10 cm) per year, you get 3000 liters of water (30 x 100 = 3000). That's a lot of water!

Place a barrel below the drain spout to catch water and cover to prevent evaporation. Smart growers store as many barrels as convenient, and keep a barrel under the downspout.

bloom" flowering fertilizer at the end of August when long nights induced flowering. All the fertilizers they used contained chelated iron.

Many hydroponic fertilizer manufacturers mix specific fertilizers for heavily mineralized water. They have a minimum volume requirement and supply the mix in liquid or wettable crystal form. Growers send a water sample to these companies to have analyzed and blend a specific fertilizer for their water. These fertilizer mixes also work well in soil and alleviate nutrient problems before they occur.

Growing the Crop

Once water, fertilizer and soil problems were solved, growing the crop was very easy.

Conchita checks the plants on the rooftop terrace and balcony daily. When the soil in the containers is dry one inch from the surface, she irrigates until 10 to 20 percent of the water comes out the drainage holes. In the first two months after transplanting, the small plants needed to be fertilized only once. When the plants were two months old and growing well, she fertilized every fourth or fifth watering with ½-strength liquid fertilizer solution. Predominately Afghani *indica* plants needed less fertilizer and *sativa* plants could take more fertilizer. They leached plants religiously once a month. (See "Pruning and Bending" Chapter Four).

Marijuana quits growing at temperatures above 90 degrees F. and the rooftop terrace reaches temperatures well in excess. Felipe built a shade house on the rooftop terrace to protect plants from the scorching sun. He framed the structure and covered the roof and the largest two walls with lightweight, dense shade cloth netting. About 50 percent of the sunlight passes through the shade cloth to supply adequate light for rapid growth. He left both ends of the structure open to allow a natural breeze to cool plants. He also placed towels on the ground under pots and wet them down during the day. The moisture evaporates and cools the shade house. On extra hot days they place a fan at one end of the shade house.

Like many smart back yard gardeners, Felipe and Conchita fill barrels with tap water and set them on bricks one yard off the ground. They dissolve ammonium phosphate in barrels to settle out (flocculate) sodium and siphon irrigation water from the top. When the barrel is empty, they clean out sediment. After each watering, they fill the barrels again so any chlorine in the water dissipates into the air. They also keep one barrel under the water downspout to catch runoff rainwater from the roof. They mix any catchment rainwater with water in the other barrels to dilute the dissolved solids before irrigating.

They went to visit Conchita's grandparents and their barnyard garden every Saturday. Felipe hangs out with Conchita's grandfather, smokes joints, tells stories and waters the garden. To compensate for salty water, Felipe sprinkles a little soluble ammonium phosphate around the plant before watering. He waters each plant about two minutes, until water puddles up in the bowl and dissolves all the

Cultivating the soil surface before watering ensures even and complete water penetration.

ammonium phosphate. When the last plant is watered, he starts all over again. Watering heavily washes (leaches) the ammonium phosphate through the soil and releases any sodium.

"Before, when I dug small holes in the back yard, I had to water every day or two. If soil dried out, the roots dried out and died too.

Felipe taught me to dig big holes and fill them with good soil that holds water and drains, too. The plants like it and so do I," said Conchita with a stunning stoned smile.

The plants in the mountains rely on natural rainfall and moisture that condenses in the mulch. Rainfall there is sporadic. Crop harvests depend on how much rainfall is received. A good year is when they harvest from 30 to 50 grams per plant. Low rainfall years, they harvest 10 to 30 grams of dried buds from each female.

Pests and Disease

Along the sea and ocean, in old fishing cities and villages, moist maritime air fills the lowlands and is drawn to the brick and stone buildings. Fungus and insects thrive in these damp, humid microclimates. In the mountains, there are winds that whip plants around and dry them out. Leaves transpire (shed moisture) to protect plants, causing more moisture to be drawn from roots. This extra stress makes weaker plants an easy target for insects and disease. Temperatures seldom dip below freezing and insect population life cycles are seldom interrupted.

Conchita and Felipe inspect plants weekly for signs of pest and fungus damage. They also check with other local flower and vegetable gardeners to see if they are having problems. When inspecting for insects and mites, they check leaves top and bottom for stippling from mites and damage from chewing insects and snails. If they see any insects or damage, they first identify the pest and wait a week to see if the damage escalates before taking action. See "Pests and Disease" in the Appendix.

To control insects, Conchita uses several old family remedies. She hand picks off as many large caterpillars and snails as she sees. If damage persists, she uses a homemade spray (See Appendix).

Mites are usually the biggest problem among sucking insects. Caterpillars cause the most problems among chewing insects. They follow the control measures in the Appendix.

Powdery mildew forms if conditions are right. Gray mold (botrytis) attacks the buds during humid warm fall days. Consult the Appendix for description of the disease and control measures.

Spring Harvest

"Next year, I'm growing a spring crop, just like Josete did down south," said Felipe excitedly, "It's so easy, I can't wait to try it. He planted clones indoors on December first. On February 15, Josete moved them into a small greenhouse insulated with Styrofoam around the perimeter to keep it warmer. He grows the cuttings about four weeks, until the weather warms outside. Up north where we live, I will have to bring them in at night to protect them from the cold. Josete transplants the cuttings into 6-liter pots of commercial potting soil and keeps them on the balcony. The days are short (10 – 11 hours) and clones start to flower. By the middle of April, he is harvesting ripe buds!"

Days are the exact same length as nights on Vernal Equinox (March 21st). From this point forward in the Northern Hemisphere, days grow longer and nights shorter. Plants that start to flower the first of March, can be harvested from mid to late April. If they do not show signs of finishing flowering by the second week in April, growers cover them with dark plastic bags or dark boxes. Spring light levels are lower and buds are smaller.

Plants for a spring crop should be one or two feet tall when moved outside. If plants are too short, less than a foot tall, the harvest will be very, very small.

Second Crops

Growers harvest spring crops and leave about 20 percent of the lower foliage on plants so they can harvest again in the fall. They cut entire branches/buds from the plants and leave the bottom branches with a few buds and foliage. As the days get longer, the plants grow more new vegetative growth and continue to grow bigger leaves throughout the summer. When the days once again grow short and nights long in the fall, the plants flower a second time.

Or in non-freezing climates, growers can harvest plants in late fall and let them winter over outdoors or in a greenhouse. If plants suffer too much temperature or moisture stress, they may die. The plants must receive supplemental light at night so plants will start vegetative growth and not flower. For best results, give plants HP sodium light so they receive a total of 18 hours of sunlight and HP sodium light every 24 hours. The extra light tricks the flowered females into reverting back to vegetative growth. Continue to give rejuvenated crops extra light until the first of March when they can resume flowering under natural sunlight. Rejuvenated plants will flower mid to late April.

Give the partly harvested females a dose of a high-nitrogen fertilizer to promote green, leafy growth. This will help harvested branches to revert to vegetative growth in 6-8 weeks.

Perpetual Harvest

An outdoor perpetual harvest is possible when integrated with an indoor mother/clone room. Simply keep a batch of clones growing in the mother room. As needed, move one to several clones outdoors into a greenhouse. Cover the greenhouse so it receives only 12 hours of darkness per day and plants flower in 7 to 12 weeks depending on variety.

Harvest

"The hardest part about harvesting is waiting until it is ready. Even after growing for more than 20 years, it's hard to wait until the buds are completely ripe to harvest," said Felipe while playing with a pair of razor sharp pruners. "That's why I sacrifice one or two plants for an early harvest. This way I get early smoke and don't hack down the crop too early."

See "Harvest" Chapter Four

This automatic darkening device is a big container on wheels. Two loops on either side support a black curtain that opens and closes every 12 hours.

Hot, Cold, Humid Interior Climate
– Midwest USA, Inland Europe

Introduction

Big Steve is a biker who grew up in the heart of the corn belt. He left the family farm and moved to the city in the mid 80's where he works as a welder. On the weekends, he fires up his Harley Knucklehead and rides to his country cabin hideaway.

Every year he starts plants from seed under a 400-watt metal halide lamp. In a couple of months the seeds grow into strong seedlings. He takes the unsexed seedlings on a country ride to find a new home. Big Steve's secret to success is his ability to find discrete hiding places and keep a crop going until harvest. Access to the mountain garden patch is via a trail that takes about 30 minutes to walk.

Steve may not harvest the absolute-best quality crop every year because he uses seeds from plants he crosses haphazardly. See discussion on Breeding and Crossing, Chapter Five.

He grows a small crop of *sinsemilla* in a backyard greenhouse. He buys artificial hibiscus, gardenia, and rose flowers with wire stems at a crafts warehouse. Big Steve attaches the flowers to the plants in the greenhouse. The greenhouse is also obscured by translucent plastic.

"I'm careful about how I attach the flowers. Got to do it right, don't want them to look overdone. I found a book at the library with photos of all the flowers I use. I use them as a guide to make the flowers look real," said Big Steve, with the conviction of an orchid grower!

The backyard garden gets out of hand. The weather is so hot and perfect that the plants grew like crazy in previous years. This year he chose smaller varieties with a heavy yield.

Site Selection

Big Steve is too smart to plant on his own land. He rents a country cabin and always plants on public property or other people's property. Each year he plants in new locations. He likes to plant in low-traffic spaces among small trees and bushes. Steve also found two different farm fields that have been out of production for a few years. He has had good crops along rivers and streams, but lost crops to floods twice in the last 10 years. When he planted along rivers, he made sure the plants were not visible from the river. Some years

Steve planted in buckets in rocky inaccessible terrain. He doesn't need to prepare the soil, he just brings in grow bags and fills them with soil on the way. The plants don't grow as big, but are seldom seen because they are growing where nobody goes or would expect them to be. Plants receive good sunlight on rocky hillsides in untillable soil. A site in dense, short bush, like sticker bushes, is another favorite spot. The sticker bushes grow high enough to prevent people from seeing through them and also serve as a deterrent from people and large animals wandering into the site.

"One of my favorite tricks is to plant where there are lots of mosquitoes," said Steve with a snicker, "If I can find a place with wasps, too. That's a double whammy. I think the best site I ever found was next to a skunk's den, around a skunk spray. I had to smear the inside of my nose with Vick's Vapor Rub to keep from smelling the skunk spray. Nobody went around there!"

"I plant deep inside patches of poison oak, poison ivy or my favorite: stinging nettles. I save seeds and broadcast them. I just cover any exposed skin with a slick rain suit and gloves to protect me. I wash the suit afterward to get rid of the oils. It's a great way to keep lightweights away from the patch!" said Steve with a smirk, "if there's a thief that wants my plants, it will cost them!"

Ideal "trails" are "invisible," have dense undergrowth and lots of sunlight. Growers walk up river and creek beds to avoid detection. Rapid plant growth will erase any damage to the vegetation between trips. Some growers lightly fertilize their trail if they use it more than a few times, but are careful – wild plants are easy to overfertilize. Other growers never take the same path to their gardens and do everything possible to avoid damaging foliage. In late summer and early fall, damaged foliage usually will not regrow. Big Steve always asks himself: Can I see the trail I just made? If not, great, if so hide it! The more difficult it is for you to get to the site, the less likely someone else will try.

Growers who think ahead bring any supplies they need – lengths of PVC pipe, gasoline-powered pumps, water tanks, soil, etc. – early in the spring before underbrush has matured and hide the supplies until needed. Sheltering also protects lightweight plastic from ultraviolet light damage.

Good soil can be in short supply on remote hillsides and is often the richest where grassland vegetation is found. Grasslands recycle nutrients in the soil and form rich fertile topsoil. (See "Soil" in Appendix).

"I order bricks of coconut fiber from out in California. Those bricks are great. They are compact and easy to carry. When I break them up and add water they expand to several times their size," said Steve, showing me how he loads them into his backpack.

A nearby water source makes a grower's life easier and safer. Growers trample foliage and risk being spotted when hauling water. The more trips, the more noticeable the trail. Look for a summertime water source that does not dry up. Water consumption is determined by the weather. Dry land crops are possible if it rains once every one to four weeks.

Growers flower summer crops by covering small greenhouses to give plants 12 hours of darkness daily. Crops are ripe in 8-12 weeks.

Sunlight is less important yet essential. Five hours of direct midday sunlight per day is necessary for acceptable growth, the more the better. Growers who scout sites during winter months visualize how trees will shade the landscape and the higher path the sun will make in the spring and summer.

Flowering females stand out like a neon sign if surrounding foliage dies back before harvest.

If you can have exclusive access to your marijuana patch by boat, you can cut potential traffic substantially.

Security

The police find hundreds of thousands of *cannabis* plants annually with aerial surveillance and infrared photography. Large plots are easier to spot than small gardens.

Many communities receive federal funds to eradicate marijuana crops. Some police departments sell the property they confiscate and buy new high tech surveillance equipment, firearms, vehicles and other toys to seek out and destroy marijuana and grower's lives. Marijuana laws in many states are extremely severe. Law enforcement officials lie, cheat and steal to achieve their means. Do not trust them under any circumstances.

"Report a marijuana grower" programs with a cash reward are

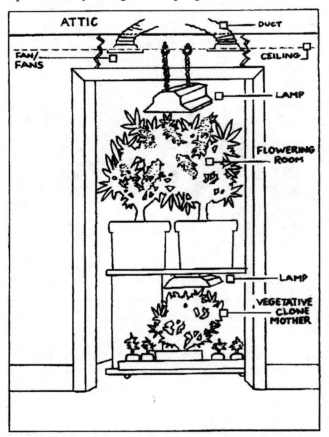

Small indoor grow room with 250-watt lamp and 2 fluorescents.

common in the USA. Six armed and dangerous narcs came to search my home on the word of a snitch. The narcs would not tell me who squealed on me or why, or if the weasel even existed. If anyone knows or even suspects you are growing marijuana, they have tremendous authority over you. A vindictive enemy can also turn you in with no evidence, even if you are not growing! Growers avoid jealous lovers, family members or malicious "friends". One of the saddest cases I saw was a daughter that extorted money from her father. The father grew marijuana to ease the pain of his glaucoma. His daughter threatened to have him arrested if he did not sell some of the crop to pay her off.

When selecting a site, remember there might be hunters (archers, black powder, rifle and shotgun) as well as mushroom and marijuana hunters or other passers by. Check all the regulations if hunting is popular in your area. The patch will have to be hidden from other wilderness users. There also might be dirt bikers or four wheel vehicles lurking.

A year round water source can be pumped uphill to water the crop. Growers are careful to bury or remove hose.

Site Preparation

Security is the number one concern in site preparation. Well concealed gardens are harvested, detected plants are not.

Prepare growing sites up to 6 months before planting. For best results, let your amended soil sit for at least a month before planting.

If the site is on an incline, planting holes must be terraced into the hillside. Make sure the terrace is large enough to catch any runoff water. Make extra gulleys to catch runoff water and channel it to the growing plant. Make a dish around the planting hole to retain water.

In heavy brush, clear a few patches so plants get enough sunlight and plant 3-6 plants in each location. When preparing the soil, I cut back all roots from competing plants and till the planting holes 2 - 3 feet square.

Soil along a riverbank is almost always fertile sandy loam. Hide the potential garden from river traffic as well as hikers and fishermen.

More sunlight is available near the tops of the trees in dense forest. Ingenious growers use deer/elk hunting stands to grow in trees. They set up a pulley system to lift a large container and potting soil up to sit on the plant stand. Install an irrigation hose from the bottom of the tree directly to the plant. The grower passes by weekly with water and manual or battery operated pump to lift water to the plant high in the tree.

A partner is necessary to work on the ground while the other person works in the tree. Smart growers use a safety line and belt and do not spend more than 4 hours off the ground in one day. Accidents happen to tired climbers.

Growing the Crop

"I pump weights and eat right, that's how I got be Big Steve. There are no big secrets, it's basic stuff. Plants are the same. I just give them what they want," said Big Steve. "You'll like this fresh squeezed orange juice. Here."

Once established in rich soil with plenty of sunshine, seedlings start producing strong vegetative growth. They produce as much vegetative or green, leafy growth as light air, nutrients and water permit. Properly maintained, marijuana will grow from ½ to 2" per day. If the plant is stunted now, it could take weeks to recover. A strong, unrestricted root system is essential to supply much needed water and nutrients. Unrestricted vegetative growth virtually guarantees a heavy harvest. The larger a plant gets, the faster the soil will dry out. A larger root system is able to take in more water and nutrients. Strong side branches are produced. They will soon be filled with flower buds.

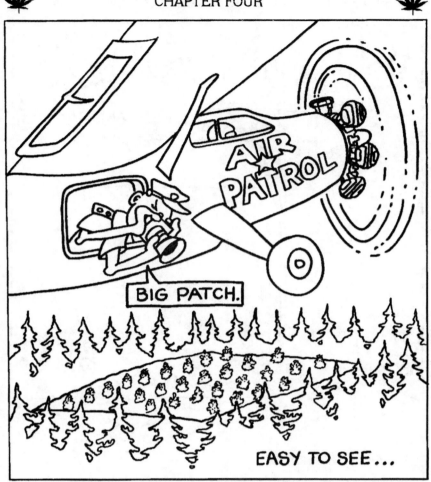

Law enforcement and thieves use aerial surveillance to spot large patches.
Small green patches in a brown, dry landscape are also easy to see.

"It's tough for a guerilla grower to be there all the time and give plants everything they need. That's why soil preparation and planting are so important. Once established, my plants can take a lot of abuse and still grow well. With luck they suffer no stress and have a good year with plenty of rain and few pest attacks, and I harvest a killer crop," said Big Steve as he showed me one of his famous beefsteak tomatoes. "I grow tomatoes in the back yard to keep me tuned-in with what is going on at the guerilla patch. If insects or dry weather stress out the tomatoes, the pot patch is probably stressing out and I need to take action."

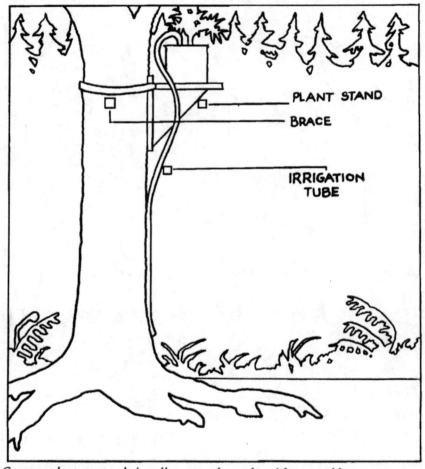

Growers plant on stands in tall trees and pass by with a portable pump to irrigate.

Pruning and Bending

Bend for security – disguise plants in the garden by making it into a hedge.

Bending and pruning change the growth pattern of *cannabis*, affecting physical shape, liquid flow and hormone concentration. Pruning strongly affects the plant, while bending has more subtle affects. When a branch is pruned off, new branches grow from the nodes just below the cut. This does not mean the plant will grow twice as much. A branch amputation is not going to make it grow faster or add any more foliage.

Bending is similar to pruning. Bending alters the flow of hormones, but unlike pruning, it does not remove them. It is much

Growers tie overhead branches together to obscure the view and still allow sunlight to pass through to plants.

easier on plants than pruning. To bend a branch, lean it in the desired direction and tie it in place. Branches can take a lot of bending before they pinch over or break. Even if a branch folds, tie it in place, it will heal itself. Young pliable branches bend much better than old, stiff ones. Bending branches horizontally encourages the to grow vertically towards the sun. Buds that receive more light turn into impressive tops.

Use wire ties or string to tie down bent plants. Plastic-coated electronic and telephone cable wire also work as well as wire ties. Leave the stem breathing room, if a stem is tied too tight, the liquids can not flow. . .

When bending, be gentle, even though *cannabis* can take much abuse. Sometimes a crotch will separate or a branch will fold over, cutting off fluid flow. These mishaps are easily fixed with a small wooden splint snugly secured with wire ties or duct tape to support the split and broken stem.

Pruning makes a plant grow bushier. The lower branches develop more rapidly when the terminal (central) bud is removed. Removing the terminal bud alters the concentration of growth inhibiting hormones. These hormones (auxins) prevent the lateral buds from growing very fast. The further a branch is from hormones at the plant tip, the less effect the auxins have. This is why, when left unpruned, *cannabis* will grow into the classic Christmas tree shape.

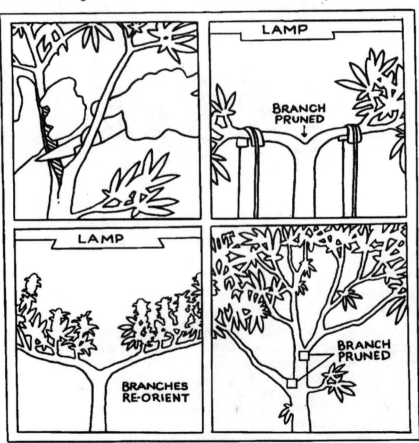

Some growers split a plant down the middle and stretch each branch out horizontally to camouflage it as a low-growing hedge. Once bent, branches and leaves reorient toward the sun. Pruning to several main stems makes plants easier to hide, but pruning does not make plants grow a heavier harvest.

Always use clean instruments when pruning; sterilize pruners, etc. by dipping in alcohol.

There are three basic methods or techniques of pruning marijuana. In the first method, the bottom branches are pruned off plants that are over 3 - 5' tall. This concentrates floral hormones so tops at the ends of branches are stronger and thicker.

In the second method, tops are pinched back. This diffuses floral hormones, making plants bushier. Pruning a plant when it is one or two months old and again at 2 or 3 months, will make it bushier. Continual pruning will keep marijuana hedge-like in shape. Pruning too much over a period of time may alter the hormonal balance so much that the plant produces spindly growth and weak flower tops. It can also retard flowering. Prune or pinch back tops one or two months before flowering starts. Pruning when pistils are set retards flowering.

Removing all but a few main branches is another method. The central bud is removed above the four branches which are left intact. This concentrates the floral hormones in the four main branches. Fewer branches are stronger and bear heavier flowers. The seedling or clone is generally two months old when the four main branches are selected. The branches selected are usually the first four that grew and the strongest.

Leaves are the factories that produce food for plants. A rumor started about how removing large shade leaves would supply more light to smaller growing tips, making them grow faster. This is bad gardening! A plant needs all the leaves it can get to produce the maximum amount of chlorophyll. Removing leaves slows chlorophyll production and stunts growth.

Removing the leaves stresses the plant. Stress is a growth inhibitor. Only leaves that are clearly dead, bug or fungus infected should be removed. Leaf removal is not pruning, it is hacking up a normally healthy plant.

Prune off lower branches that have spindly, sickly growth. When pruning, cut off the entire branch. Pruning the lower branches has a minimal effect on floral hormone concentration.

"Sometimes I run out of smoke and stop by to check the plants out and get some smoke too," said Big Steve with a gleam in his eye.

Pruning for Smoke

Marijuana increases in potency as it grows older. A notable increase in potency is evident when tops set white hair-like pistils.

Potency peaks out eight to 16 weeks later. Desperate growers pick early smoke by pinching off growing shoots (most potent) or picking leaves (less potent). Other growers remove entire branches or plants. Pinching off tops diffuses floral hormones, sending them back to lower branches. Snipping tips also causes a new set of branches to grow below the cut. Big Steve has so much marijuana stored from last year that he does not think of snipping tips.

Harvest

Once large leaves are fully formed, THC potency has generally peaked out in that leaf. Healthy green leaves retain peak potency.

Harvest leaves if they show signs of disease or rapid yellowing that fertilizer has failed to cure. Once they start to yellow and die, potency declines. Large fan leaves often yellow just before tops are ripe.

Marijuana needs water throughout life. Withholding water to stress plants before harvest should only be done during the last few days, if done at all.

The size of the plant has little to do with maturity. Outdoors, a plant might reach a height of over ten feet (3 yards) and still not be ready for harvest, or be in full flower when only a few inches tall.

Some growers harvest at night to limit exposure to other hikers. Transporting freshly cut *cannabis* is more comfortable at night, especially if there are no barking dogs. Wary growers find out when the police change shift and harvest at that time. If a local resident or passerby calls the police, it will take time while the officer is dispatched to investigate. A sharp pocket knife will reduce the amount of material they must carry at harvest time. Some growers remove large fan leaves a couple of days before harvesting to speed transport. Loading the harvest in a backpack facilitates transport and protects the crop from detection. If harvesting several different varieties, put each in a separate bag before packing in the backpack.

Avoid harvesting in the rain. Excessive moisture is the perfect environment for fungus. The dryer the plants at the harvest, the better.

Different Varieties

Varieties not acclimated to latitudes, such as Colombian or Jamaican, are best left to late October, or even mid November if the weather permits.

The size and age of the plant has little to do with maturity. How quickly a plant flowers depends on the amount of darkness it receives every 24 hours, that determines when it flowers, not length of time needed to mature the flowers. Typically, *cannabis* changes from vegetative growth to flowering when the light per day drops below 12 – 14 hours. In general a seedling needs to be 60 days old before it will mature into an adult. Clones will flower even if they have been rooted less than 60 days.

Pure *sativa* varieties take longer to mature than pure *indica* types. There are numerous varieties available that are a cross of both *indica* and *sativa*. Sometimes *cannabis* ruderalis is bred into the seed. At peak of florescence buds have the most fragrant odor. As senescence sets in, the bouquet dissipates from the fragrance.

When to Harvest

Peak ripeness depends on bud development, weather, and fungus. While thieves and law enforcement can influence decision of when to harvest. The weather may force an early harvest. Watch weather reports for freezing weather fronts. A mild frost (temperatures of 31 – 32 degrees F. for an hour or two) or even temperatures down to 35 or 40 degrees F. will slow growth for several days. A killing frost will wipe out a crop in an hour or less. Frozen plants look and smoke like boiled spinach. Watch out for cool damp conditions that foster fungus and force an early harvest.

Harvest plants in farmers' fields before the farm crop. Find out when the harvest occurred last year and when it is planned this year. Planting early-maturing varieties is smart. Get a copy of the local hunting regulations and talk to residents to find out when hunters roam the fields so you can avoid them.

If there is an early, light, frost when buds are small; some

Use pruners to harvest plants and leave the root ball in the ground.

growers gamble and let the buds finish maturing rather than harvesting a small quantity of premature bud.

Immediately moving the harvested crop to a safe drying location will ensure minimum damage to the delicate buds. If the freshly cut *cannabis* is left in a wet bundle for more than a few hours, the chances of mold* increase.

Male Harvest

Male flowers take from 2 - 4 weeks to mature their pollen bearing pods from the time they first emerge. Watch out for early openers. They continue producing flowers for several weeks after the first pods have begun to shed pollen. Once male flowers are clearly visible, but before they have opened, is the time of peak THC production and the best time to harvest even though males have much less THC than females they do have some. The degradation process accelerates as flowers develop and fall.

To avoid pollination, growers put a plastic bag over male plants at harvest if close to females. Keep males totally isolated from flowering females by moving a mile or more away. Indoors under a light is best. The ability to produce viable pollen does not change in this environment.

Harvesting most of the branches, leaving only one or two pollen bearing branches, usually supplies enough pollen. One male flower contains enough pollen to fertilize many female ovules. A few clusters of male flowers produce enough pollen for most breeding projects.

Male harvest may be prolonged by harvesting flowers with small scissors or fingernails as they emerge. After plucking off male flowers, new ones soon appear. New male flowers are ripe when the females are in full bloom. Missing a few male flowers is easy in this time consuming process.

*Once there is a trace of gray mold, harvest immediately and cut out and throw away moldy bits. This moldy weed is extremely unhealthy for growers or their customers to smoke!

Sinsemilla Harvest

Sinsemilla flowers are mature from 6 – 12+ weeks after flowering starts

The best time to harvest *sinsemilla* is when THC production has peaked, but not yet started the degradation process. Lower flower tops that received less light might be a little slower in maturing. *Indica* and *indica/sativa* varieties tend to go through 5 – 10 weeks of rapid bud formation before leveling off. The harvest is taken 1 - 3 weeks after growth slows. Harvest in most commercial *indica* varieties is ready all at once, in 8 - 12 weeks.

Sativa varieties tend to form buds at an even rate throughout flowering, with no marked decline in growth rate. With these varieties, buds at the top of the plant may reach peak potency a few days to a couple of weeks before buds on lower branches. They may require several harvests. Long season plants, such as Thai, can flower for several months.

Smoking, diminishing returns and scientific observation are three excellent methods used to test for peak ripeness. Smoking is the most fun. Harvest an average bud, dry it at 200 degrees F for 10 - 15 minutes and smoke it. The smoke will probably be harsh, but palatable. Make the test when straight and several times throughout flowering. This method lets the high decide the best time to harvest.

Diminishing returns is a point that is reached when the pistils on the bottom of the bud are dying (turning brown) at a faster rate than they are growing from the top of the bud. At this point, THC production has usually peaked out and on its way down hill. This method is the best way to tell a ripe bud with the naked eye.

Looking at resin glands with an inexpensive microscope (20 – 50X) is the easiest precise way to tell when THC production has reached its peak. Take a small, thin, resinous portion of the bud and place it under the microscope at low magnification (30X). A

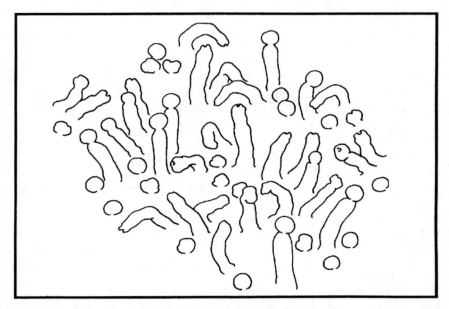

Resin glands are easy to see with a 30X microscope. Peak harvest is when half of the stalked resin glands are translucent and half turn amber.

flashlight or lamp helps provide top light for an unshadowed view of the resin glands. Portable microscopes afford a quick peek at resin glands without harvesting the bud. Look for three kinds of glands. The glands with the knob at the top (1) (capitate-stalked trichomes) have the highest concentration of THC. Other glands, (2) bulbous and (3) stalked glands or trichomes contain much less THC.

Preference dictates harvest time. Once capitate-stalked trichomes develop a head, are fully developed and still translucent, it is the peak of an early harvest. When the glands turn amber they are decomposing and THC content declines. Resin glands do not develop all at the same instant, therefore some glands will be changing to translucent and others decomposing. Peak harvest is when more glands are translucent than amber. Check over a period of several days and check several buds from different plants to make sure the maximum amount of capitate-stalked trichomes are ripe for harvest.

Growers report a soaring high if buds are picked a little early, when more resin glands are translucent and a heavier more lethargic stone when buds are picked after more resin glands are amber. The harvest can gain quite a bit of weight when buds are left to mature a little longer.

Harvest Step-by-Step

Step One: Stop fertilizing and leach plants 2 – 4 weeks before harvest to avoid fertilizer taste.

Step Two: Harvest branches/buds individually at peak ripeness if they mature at different rates.

Step Three: Harvest entire plant if ripe by cutting near the base with clippers. Jerking roots is unnecessary. THC is produced in the foliage, not roots. One grower was arrested with only roots and soil as evidence. Remember to destroy all roots to avoid problems.

Step Four: Harvest near the end of the day to allow a full, sunny day for active resin production.

Step Five: Drying the entire plant by hanging upside down is convenient. When stems are left intact, drying is much slower. Leaving all the larger leaves on the tops acts as a protective shield to flower buds. Tender resin glands are protected from rupture or loss.

Step Six: Method A. Cut each branch into lengths of 6 - 24", cutting away all leaves with clippers or scissors. Hang the branches in a dark well ventilated room at temperatures of 60 – 70 degrees F. until dry. Once dry, cut the tops from branches, taking special care to handle the tender tops as little as possible.

Method B. Harvest the entire plant by cutting it off at the base, then hang it upside down. Wait for it to dry before removing any fan leaves or manicuring the tops. A little THC may be lost, since the tender tops are more susceptible to bruises and rupture once they are dry. Use this method in warm climates to slow drying and mellow the smoke.

Step Seven: Growers also remove the leaves one or two days before actually cutting the plants at the base. Harvesting large leaves early speeds drying time.

Step Eight: To manicure the tops after drying, snip away any leaves not covered with resin and remove buds from the main stem.

Step Nine: After manicuring, package the tops in a rigid container, like a glass jar, to preserve the resin glands.

Step Ten: Budget about 6-10 hours per pound for harvest and manicure.

Drying

Drying converts THC from its non-psychoactive acid form to its psychoactive neutral form. Drying also converts 75 percent or more of the freshly harvested plant into water vapor and other gases.

When harvested, the THC (tetrahydrocannabinol – the active ingredient in *cannabis* that gets you high) content starts to degrade. Light, heat (above 90 degrees F), friction from fondling hands and damp, humid conditions all degrade THC.

THC is produced in the leaves and flowers. Stems and roots but contain few cannabinoids, if any, and the resin is not very psychoactive. Boiling roots to extract THC is crazy and does not work. Hanging plants upside down is for convenience, not to let resin drain into the buds.

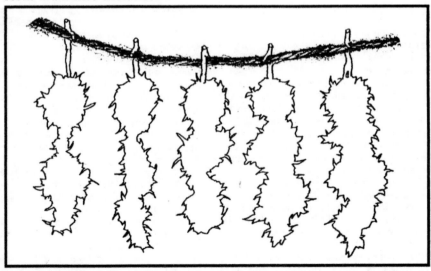

Plants dry evenly when hung from drying lines in a cool dark room.

Key to Photos in Color Section - Pages 1 - 3

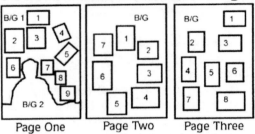

Page One   Page Two   Page Three

Page ONE

1) Sean selling seeds for Marc Emery Seeds Direct in Vancouver, BC Canada.

2) Sensi Seeds and Greenhouse Seeds are two of the biggest sellers at the Amsterdam Café located in downtown Vancouver, BC, Canada.

3) Seeds in water soaking overnight.

4) Female plants have two early white hair-like pistils that grow from branch internodes.

5) Signs of an early male plant include a single spur and small pollen sack that grows from branch internodes. A visible pollen sack is the only sure way to tell he's a boy.

6) Growers cut branch tips and hold them in a bucket of water while they are waiting to turn into clones.

7) Next, the cutting is dipped in a rooting hormone.

8) Clone is then inserted into rooting medium.

9) "Stuck" or rooted clone after two weeks of rooting.

Upper Background: Flat or tray of recently rooted clones.

Lower Background: Rooted clones in Switzerland sell for $5 to $10 US each.

Page TWO

1) Excess fertilizer or salt in water burn leaf tips. Yellowing between leaf veins (chlorosis) is caused by lack of iron. Remedy by flushing soil with large amount of water to wash out excess (fertilizer) salts and apply chelated micronutrients containing iron.

2) All leaves came from the same garden and suffer from the same problem, excessive salt in the water. The water is rich in sodium, calcium and other salts that cause many nutrients to become unavailable. The solution, flush soil heavily each month with water to wash out excess salts.

3) Severely overfertilized plant has curled under leaves. Remedy by flushing soil heavily each week with water. Resume fertilization after 3 to 4 weeks.

4) Deep purple small leaves indicate lack of potassium. This micro-nutrient is locked out because of excess sodium in irrigation water. Remedy by flushing soil heavily with water. Foliar feed with all purpose N-P-K fertilizer about two weeks after flushing. Flush plants heavily every month to wash away toxic salt build-up.

5) Chlorosis is caused by a lack of iron. Without available iron, nitrogen becomes unavailable. Leaves yellow between veins. Remedy by flushing soil heavily with water

Page TWO (continued...)

and add chelated iron to water.

6) A lack of magnesium causes leaf fringes to turn brown and curl along with brownish blotches. To cure, flush soil with water and add sulfate of magnesium (Epsom salts).

7) Early signs of magnesium deficiency are brown blotches. This leaf also shows signs of other trace element deficiencies. Remedy by flushing soil heavily with water to wash out excess salts that lock out magnesium and other trace elements.

Background: More than 100 slimy slugs were attracted to this saucer filled with stale beer. Attracted to the sugar and yeast, mollusks enter for a quick drink and drown.

Page THREE

1) Bending plants keeps them from growing above the fence, out of neighbors view.

2) Short squat indica plant on Paris, France balcony received filtered sun behind bamboo wall and produced 1.5 ounces of choice buds.

3) A tall painted bamboo wall shields this garden from sight, except for helicopters that trespass and satellite fotos that infringe on citizens privacy.

4) German grower sets plants outdoors every day for 12 hours of summer sun. He returns home in the afternoon and moves them into a dark room. This shot was taken on August first after 7 weeks of flowering.

5) Lola is this little girl's name. Lola's root system was baked and stunted by Spanish sunshine. At harvest she was 5 months old and only 6 inches tall.

6) Starting in mid July, this grower moved plants from the sunny balcony daily to a dark closet to give 12 hours. Plants finished flowering by mid September.

7) Plant on same Paris balcony as above grew faster and needed more fertilizer. Note slightly yellow leaves caused by low nitrogen level. Plant yielded two ounces of prime bud.

8) Hot sun heats the buckets and roots to more than 120 degrees F. The heat caused root growth to slow and diminished harvest by half.

Background: Huge 'Jack Herer' bud matured in grower's back yard. This plant yielded 10 ounces of dried mature bud.

Seeds

Sex

THE AMSTERDAM COFFEE SHOP
GASTOWN VANCOUVER, B.C.
CANADA

Cloning

Problems

Roofs
Terraces &
Balconies

Back Yards

Swiss
Breeder

Harvest
&
Drying

Key to Photos in Color Section - Pages 4 - 8

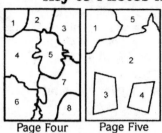

Page Four   Page Five

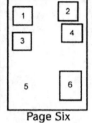

Page Six

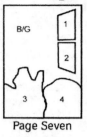

Page Seven

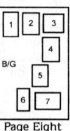

Page Eight

Page FOUR

1) Healthy marijuana crop flanked by pampas grass add extra texture and ambience to this European back yard landscape.

2) The grower removed large yellowing leaves from this bent plant to facilitate harvest. Sunshine heated this black pot which stunted root growth diminishing harvest.

3) Marijuana plants blend into the landscape in the entrance of this grower's Mediterranean home.

4) Smiling grower in Amsterdam backyard, located 30 feet below sea level, reflects his joy of gardening in a free country.

5) Sativa/indica cross in late September just days from harvest.

6) Just half of this 'White Widow' plant in Spanish back yard is visible. It yielded just over a pound of manicured buds.

7) 'Jack Herer' produces thick dense buds outdoors.

8) Spanish grower shares a stoned smile with his sativa crop.

Page FIVE

1) Low-growing plants mature early and blend in with bright yellow flowers in this British garden.

2) Background: Spanish variety 'Ja ja' produces one of the most soaring sativa highs available. Note the characteristic narrow sativa leaves on plant that just started to flower.

3) Blooming plants in this remote Spanish garden mix well with surrounding foliage, making casual detection difficult.

4) This low-growing flowering sativa sinsemilla nestled in a corn field receives less sunlight and is virtually impossible to see from the air or ground.

Page SIX

1) Hundreds of seedlings are started in flats to grow a large gene pool.

2) Thousands of plants are moved outdoors from the greenhouse to harden-off.

3) Scores of clones and seedlings are started in the greenhouse before moving outdoors.

4) Crop of clones shows even uniform growth.

5) Background: An HP sodium lamp adds extra

Page SIX (continued...)

lumens to subdued natural light in greenhouse.

6) Large healthy clone is planted outdoors early in the spring to compensate for cool climate. Note many trees have not yet grown leaves.

Page SEVEN

1) This Greenhouse Seed Company variety has naturally occurring purple leaves.

2) Sativa/indica cross is nearing peak potency. Observe the white pistils are turning brown. Depending on taste, growers harvest when about half the pistils have turned brown.

3) Ripe sativa 'Ja Ja' bud is soaring toward the sun.

4) Spanish grower peeks through last year's buds. Plants were bent causing each bud to grow upright toward the sun.

Background: Spanish 'Ja Ja' sinsemilla in full bloom.

Page EIGHT

1) Swiss "Smelling Bag", flanked by author's German edition of *Indoor Marijuana Horticulture*, is stuffed with prime buds. Swiss law allowed buds to be sold as "Smelling Bags". Clients purchase the sealed bags, take them home and "smell" them, not!

2) Spanish grower labors under warm sunshine to harvest more than 30 huge plants in his backyard garden.

3) Entire plants are hang and dry in a cool dark Spanish shed.

4) Stressing plants by withholding water slows growth and reduces harvest substantially.

5) A box of manicured buds is gently stirred daily until dry. Buds dried in 5 days in conditions of 60 percent humidity and 55 to 65-degree F. temperatures.

6) Huge 9-month-old Thai trunk dwarfs ballpoint pen.

7) Grower protects plants in newspaper to control temperature and humidity. He also keeps notes - plant variety, drying date, etc. - noted on the paper.

EXTRA PHOTO - Background - Picture of dried Afghani Kush hybrid grown in an Amsterdam yard. Photo by G. Curtis.

Buds dry in a forced air food preserver in less than 24 hours. A green raspy chlorophyll taste permeates the resulting fast-dried smoke. Growers who are in a hurry to smoke place a few buds in the microwave and turn it on in short, weak bursts of 15 - 30 seconds each. Recycle until dry. The smoke is harsh but effective. It will take 10 - 15 minutes at 200 degrees F. when using a gas, electric or a toaster oven. Fast-dried marijuana is raspy and harsh. Temperatures above 200 degrees F will vaporize THC.

For best results, drying should be slow and incorporate circulating, temperate (40 - 60 degrees F.), dry air. When dried slowly, over 2 - 3 weeks, moisture evaporates evenly into the air, yielding uniformly dry buds with minimal THC decomposition. These buds smoke smooth and taste sweet. Quickly dried buds burn hot and taste harsh. Tops dried too slowly in humid air (above 80 percent) tend to contract fungus and burn poorly.

Big Steve hangs tops from drying lines near the ceiling in a dark room with an oscillating fan on the floor to dry. Other growers tack plywood together to form a small room, use a large cardboard box, or stretch strings between the walls to form drying lines. Circulate the air in the room/box with an oscillating fan. Fungus can become a problem, especially if ventilation is inadequate. Keep constant lookout for any signs of fungus. Light hastens resin decomposition. Big Steve never lets the fan blow directly on the drying plants; it dries them too fast.

Light, heat and friction start the biodegradation process and are dry and drying marijuana's biggest enemies. Keep dried marijuana off hot car dash boards, radiators, refrigerators, etc. Friction also destroys tender resin glands. Baggies and fondling hands rupture tiny resin glands. To keep dried marijuana in mint condition, store it in an air tight, rigid container and place it in the refrigerator. Do not keep it in the freezer, very cold temperatures combined with moisture destroy the THC glands. Canning jars allow buds to be admired and protected. Jars are very popular to contain the fragrance of pungent varieties. Some growers place an orange or lemon peel in the jar to add aroma to the bouquet, while others argue foreign substances degrade from taste.

Leaves dry very well in a paper bag. Throw leaves, shake and small buds in a shopping bag and fold the top over. Place the bag in a dry, warm place out of the way, like on top of the refrigerator or in a heated room. Check it every day, turning the leaves over. They should be dry in a week or two depending on humidity. The warmer the sack, the faster the marijuana dries, and the harsher it smokes.

You can also dry manicured tops in paper bags.

Cool Mountain and Prairie Climate
– Rocky Mountains, Great Plains, Switzerland

Introduction

Felix lives in a Swiss Canton (or state) on the Italian side of the Alps and has a passion for *cannabis* that saturates every cell in his body. He loves to explain in vivid detail each part of *cannabis'* life cycle. The animated story always culminates with his specialty, plant sex. Felix is a breeder.

Like most Europeans, Felix smoked exclusively imported hash, until he tasted marijuana. His first hit on a pure *cannabis* joint was more than twenty years ago back when good *cannabis* was virtually impossible to find. In 1978 he grew his first marijuana garden. The Swiss mountain climate was very harsh and his imported seed stock grew poorly in the cool climate. In 1980, Felix started to replicate milder climates by growing indoors. He thought he was on the right track, but needed confirmation. In 1982, when on a seed gathering expedition in India, he asked a Sadhu (holy man) "what is the best *cannabis* to smoke?" The Sadhu responded: "Smoke only the *cannabis* that grows in your country. Otherwise, do not smoke at all!"

Five years later, his passionate hobby evolved into a full time pursuit. Felix was growing indoors, in a greenhouse on his property located at an altitude of 300 meters (850 feet) and in several mountain gardens located at 1,300 meters (4,200 feet). By 1996 Felix had enough experience and genetic material to start the **Owl's Production*** seed company. In 1997 the company was granted a licensee by the Swiss government and Felix started to advertise his seeds internationally. His marijuana seeds are adapted to cool alpine temperatures and poor mountain soil at an altitude of 4,200 feet.

Felix's goal is to develop marijuana seeds that produce a high level of THC and low CBD and CBN levels, plus they must grow well at high altitudes and be fungus-resistant. Large per-plant yield is less important.

To accomplish his goal, Felix grows indoors and transplants seedlings and cuttings outdoors in one of two greenhouses. Later he transplants to the outdoor gardens.

Felix grows about 3,000 plants in his gardens at 4,200 feet every year. Felix's main achievement is breeding plants that grow well in this relatively harsh climate. He has developed several seed varieties that will withstand the cool, humid weather at high altitudes. Two of

*Owl's Production, via Collina 58, 6612 Ascona TI, Switzerland, Tel/Fax: +41-91-791-7823.

the strongest most cold and mold tolerant varieties are 'Grandiflora' and 'Purpurea Ticinensis', with THC contents that range from 18 to 24 percent.

This Swiss breeder speeds the natural selection process with a wary eye and a firm hand. He has one simple cure for every plant weakness: remove it from the garden and the genetic pool. Any plant that produces low THC levels, or that is susceptible to mold and insect attack, or grows poorly in cool temperatures, is banished.

Site Selection and Security

"Sneaky thieves are difficult to keep away. I have a big dog and the he chases people I do not want here away," sighed Felix. He continued, "Robbers are a big problem. I have to sleep in the field to keep the young people and junkies out of the plants. They think they can sell any plant. They take plants and don't care if they step on other plants or even if the plant is ripe!"

After robbery, security is a small issue for Felix. His neighbors and local authorities know he has a passion for top quality marijuana and that he grows it in several locations. They protect his freedom to garden and his rights as a Swiss citizen.

His main criteria for selecting garden plots is based on availability, ease of use and hours of sunshine received. The alpine soil is packed with minerals, lacks humus and has a pH of 6 to 6.5.

"In summer, there are 90 degree days. I am fortunate to grow in a special area inside of Switzerland – for example Chinese palm trees grow here. Night temperatures are cooler, 65-70 degrees. At the 4,200 foot altitude gardens, the temperature drops to 55 degrees at night. Day and night temperature stress makes plants produce more resin, but they are not as big. The plants in the mountains always have about 10-20% more THC than those in the lower gardens," said Felix.

Site Preparation and Planting

The first average frost at the 850-foot altitude is the first week of November and the last average frost date is the last week of February. Felix moves the first seedlings and cuttings to a butane-heated greenhouse the first week in March at his 850-foot location. He augments naturally low light levels in the greenhouse with 400-watt HP sodium lamps. The lights are controlled by a timer to operate in the morning and late afternoon when sunlight levels are low. The lights go off during midday hours when sunlight is strongest. The lights stay on after dark to give young plants more hours of light in the early spring and sustain vegetative growth. Plants receive a total of 14 hours of sunlight and artificial light until they are transplanted outdoors.

Felix has two greenhouses that total 90 square yards of floor space. He uses gas to heat in the winter and cool in the summer. To acclimate plants to the more severe outdoor climate, he keeps the temperature at 55 degrees at night and 78 degrees during the day.

"I give my little babies 14 hours light in the spring. By April 25th I am able to move the little plants outdoors. I make clones from the mother plant when she is growing outdoors. I grow one hectare (2.5 acres US) of 6-foot-tall plants. I keep them short and they grow very strong. They can live good with the cold weather," said Felix.

Historically, temperatures dip to freezing at the 4,200-foot gardens the first week of October and rise above freezing the first week in May. Felix normally plants on May 15th and harvests from late September to the first week in October at these high alpine gardens.

The native soil is poor and a little acidic. Felix does little to improve the structure of the poor native soil before and after

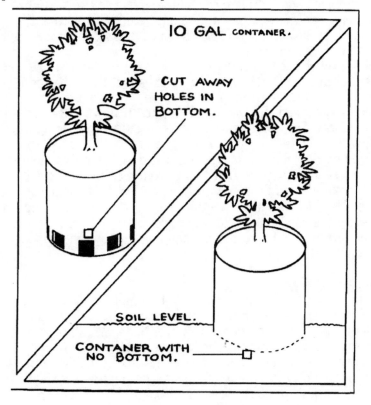

Plants grown in large 10-gallon containers with excellent drainage produce two or three times the harvest of plants in 5-gallon pots.

planting. He physically removes weeds and digs holes about 18-inches wide and 18 inches deep for each plant. He adds a handful of blood meal to the soil, covers it with 3-4 inches of soil and transplants cuttings from the greenhouse into the prepared holes on the cultivated native soil. The roots have time to get accustomed to the soil, penetrate down another 3-4 inches and hit the nitrogen-rich blood meal. After transplanting, he waters each plant heavily so roots come into firm contact with the soil.

Growing the Crop

"In the spring and fall, it rains very much. There is little rain in the summer, July and August. In September the rain comes again. It rains hard almost every year by the end of September. I want an early harvest so the rain and mold do not affect the flowers and the plant can mature. There is more rain and the temperature is cooler at the 4,200-foot garden than it is at the 850-foot garden. The gardens at 4,200 feet have good light and the sun is strong so the girls grow good. Every year, the weather is different," said Felix with an enthusiastic smile and continued, "If we have a good October (with no rain) I have a good crop."

Felix gives the tender transplants more water the first few weeks of growth, until their root system is established. Once the roots find the blood meal, they start to grow faster and he knows the root system is established. He waters when growth slows a little or when plants look dry. Dry plants have slightly wilted leaves. He waters when plants need it.

"I do not give plants much fertilizer and I do not give them much care, just like in nature. Worms in the ground cultivate the soil for me and make a little fertilizer. I grow more than 3,000 female clones every year and do not have a tractor. I spend my time watching plants and finding the good ones" said Felix with a grin. "I give the girls their last fertilizer, a handful of chicken manure to each one, on the full moon in July."

Fungus and Pests

Mold is black and white to Felix. White mold, powdery mildew, comes first. It appears with the cool, humid weather in the autumn. Black mold, *botrytis*, attacks dense flower buds. Wet, humid weather gives *botrytis* the climate it needs to start and live. The only control for *botrytis* is to cut it out and remove the affected foliage from the garden. Avoid *botrytis* by growing plants that mature early and protect the crop from humid, wet conditions.

It's tough to avoid either kind of mold: powdery mildew and *botrytis*, in a climate with constant 80 percent or higher humidity.

Success is dependent on the genetic makeup of the plant and the weather.

"If the plants grow fungus I don't want them. I have to grow strong plants and ones that are always healthy. For example, 'Haze' a pure Thai sativa, never comes ripe here. Plants in the mountains have to flower early and have much THC. Much THC is what I want. The best cross I have found is a strong *indica* mother that grows big buds and a potent *sativa* father. For example, a good 'Big Bud' mama and an 'AK-47' is a good cross," said Felix.

The local deer get to be a big problem in the spring when tender growing shoots are the most succulent foliage available. Often neighbors sheep and goats run wild in the summer and can devastate a garden in a couple of days. The dog, Fritz, is a great sentry and keeps all other animals off the property as long as he is awake.

Nocturnal deer pose a problem when Fritz is asleep, so Felix uses several of the controls listed in the Appendix to keep them at bay.

Snails also cause a lot of damage if left unattended. See Appendix for control measures.

Note: This book is about basic guerilla cultivation techniques today's marijuana growers are using. Felix, like many breeders, is a fountain of knowledge on genetics. Only the basics of breeding are covered here. For complete background on marijuana breeding, see *Marijuana Botany*, by Robert Connell Clarke. It is available in many bookstores or from Marlin's Books, 1-888-306-7187 (marijuanagrowing.com).

Flowering

Cannabis must flower to complete its annual life cycle successfully. Marijuana is a dioecious plant, being either male (pollen producing) or female (ovule producing). Hermaphrodite (bisexual) plants, with both male and female flowers on the same plant, also occur among some varieties.

The long nights and short days of autumn signal *cannabis* to start flowering. Growth patterns and chemistry change: stems elongate, leaves grow progressively fewer blades, cannabanoid production slows somewhat then accelerates; flower formation is rapid at first then slows. Green chlorophyll production, requiring much nitrogen, slows. Phosphorus uptake increases to assist floral formation.

Water during flowering is important to carry on the plant's chemistry and resin production. Withholding water to stress a plant stunts growth and decreases yield.

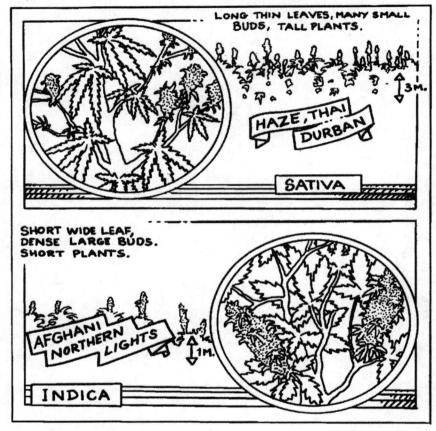

LONG THIN LEAVES, MANY SMALL BUDS, TALL PLANTS.

HAZE, THAI, DURBAN

3M.

SATIVA

SHORT WIDE LEAF, DENSE LARGE BUDS. SHORT PLANTS.

AFGHANI NORTHERN LIGHTS

1M.

INDICA

Sativa varieties have long thin leaves. Indica varieties have shorter wider leaves.

Male

Male *cannabis* plants mature before female plants. Males flower and continue to shed yellowish, dust-like pollen from bell shaped pollen sacks (flowers) well into the females flowering stage to ensure pollination. Male flowers are about ½-inch long, pastel green to yellowish. Flowers first develop near the top of the plant and hang in clusters at the base of branches. Gradually, flowers develop closer towards the bottom of the male. When fully formed, floral sacks split open, shedding pollen into the breeze. Be careful, males show up 3 weeks or more before female flowers.

Males are often tall with stout stems, sporadic branching, and fewer leaves than their female counterpart.

Male *cannabis* produces a low volume of flowers that contain virtually no THC. They also fertilize females, causing them to stop seed bract and high THC production and start seed formation.

Growers remove males, except those used for breeding, as soon as their sex has been determined, before pollen is shed. The most secure way to distinguish male plants early is to clone for sex. See "Cloning for Sex".

Removing Males: Early male varieties begin to produce flowers and pollen as soon as July in northern climates. Varieties from southern climates may not start to flower until mid-September. Growers who plant many different varieties look for males weekly from July through September (Northern Hemisphere). They remove all male plants before flowers open to ensure a *sinsemilla* crop. If just one male flower opens and sheds pollen, much of the crop could be seeded.

Female

Commonly, females grow heavier foliage with branches close together on the stem. Flowering starts gradually as day length declines. Females are prized for heavy, potent, resin production and weighty flower yield. Like the male, female flowers first appear near the top of the terminal bud and gradually develop towards the bottom of the plant. Female flowers have two small ¼ to ½-inch fuzzy, white hairs, called pistils, that form a "V". A seed bract encloses an ovule at the base of the set of pistils. Seed bracts form dense clusters of buds along the stem.

Buds usually grow rapidly for the first 4 or 5 weeks, then grow at a slower rate. Indica and indica/sativa commercial crosses finish flowering in 4 to 6 more weeks and tropical sativas can take up to 6 months to ripen completely. When the ovule has been fertilized by male pollen, rapid calyx formation and resin production slow and seed growth starts.

Sinsemilla

Sinsemilla (pronounced sin-se-miya) combines two Spanish words: *sin* without and *semilla* seed. *Sinsemilla* is used to describe flowering, female marijuana flowers that have not been fertilized by male pollen.

Sinsemilla varieties are often potent, with a high volume of THC per flower bud and all smoke. The unpollinated female remains in the flowering stage; seed bract formation and resin production peak out. More and larger seed bracts develop thicker along the stem, yielding more high quality buds.

Any female marijuana plant may become *sinsemilla*, regardless of origin, by removing the male plants. Removing males virtually guarantees that no male pollen will touch the tender pistils of the female. (See: Hemp Pollen and Hermaphrodites).

Sex reversal sometimes becomes a problem when growing only female plants. Unstable genetics and stress are the leading cause of plants that turn into hermaphrodites. These plants produce male flowers to supply fertile pollen to complete their life cycle successfully, especially if females flower past peak ripeness – 8 weeks or more. Pick off the male flowers, as soon as they appear to ensure a *sinsemilla* crop.

Some growers let this late hermaphrodite pollen fertilize females and the seeds produce mostly female offsprings. But they will also have hermaphrodite tendencies. Seeds may also be unstable breeding stock. For more information see *Marijuana Botany*.

Hermaphrodites

A hermaphrodite has both male and female flowers on the same plant. Some growers claim their seeds will produce a higher percentage of female plants. Hermaphrodites are usually avoided; their offsprings are hard to predict and control. Some hermaphrodites are 10 percent male and 90 percent female, while others are 90 percent male and 10 percent female.

Harvest and Storage

Felix harvests plants when the THC glands are at peak ripeness. See Chapter Four for more details.

Breeding - Making Plant Crosses

Cannabis seeds that are the product of many generations of selective breeding are highly prized for their potency and acclimatization to different climates. Most growers prefer seeds from an *indica/sativa* cross. These crosses show favorable growth characteristics: squat, bushy, vigorous growth, early, sustained potency, disease resistance and heavy flower yield. In nature male plants shed pollen into the wind to randomly fertilize any receptive females. Breeders add precision and control to this process. They catch pollen from a desirable male and put it in contact with chosen female pistils.

Two basic types of breeding must be understood. First, plants with the same parents and ancestry that have been crossed back with one another are inbred or true bred varieties. Second, hybrid or outbred plants include varieties with different ancestry that are crossed with one another.

Inbreeding is necessary to establish a pure breed. True or pure breed plants have common growth characteristics. If the plants are not a pure breed, it is virtually impossible to predict the outcome of hybrid plants. After the 5th to 6th generation, negative characteristics such as low potency, leggyness and lack of vigor tend to dominate. Inbreeding is necessary to establish a true breed to cross with other true breeds to make F^1 hybrid plants.

Inbreeding is used to establish relatively stable plants. The chosen females are bred back with males of the same variety. Inbreeding establishes a true breed, plants with the same growth characteristics. These plants, of known ancestry and growth characteristics, are used to breed hybrid plants.

Even after true breeding or back crossing *cannabis* for five or six generations, varieties are difficult to stabilize. The offspring of true bred parents do not always look all the same. Some varieties tend to be more stable than others. The most stable variety is Skunk #1 and is used as the male parent by countless breeders.

F^1 hybrid plants from strong, true-breeding parents have "hybrid vigor". Plants with hybrid vigor grow about 25 percent faster than non-hybrids. Seed companies continue to sell F^1 seed because of the strong genetic characteristics and the 25% increase in growth rate. An F^1 plant, grown to maturity and crossed with a different parent, results in an F2 hybrid. An F2 hybrid often looses many of its desirable qualities, including the 25% faster growth rate. Smart growers ensure strong genetic retention by transplanting clones from several strong F^1 mothers.

Seeds from self-pollinated hermaphrodite plants are inbred. Smart growers avoid self-pollinated hermaphrodites because they are normally more unstable and produce pollen.

Male pollen from hermaphrodites having only a few male flowers on a predominately female plant, may be used to cross-pollinate another female. This method may yield 75 percent or higher female offsprings. Nonetheless, when using hermaphrodite breeding stock, chances are increased of producing hermaphrodite seeds.

See *Marijuana Botany* by Robert Connell Clarke for a detailed discussion and instructions on *cannabis* breeding.

Plant Crossing Step-by-Step

Step One: Choose male breeding stock exhibiting desirable characteristics: strong smell, vigor and potency. Potency is difficult to judge in males. One ballpark measure of potency is to rub the stem between your fingers. The more the stem smells of resin, the more prone it is to be potent.

Step Two: One branch of flowers from each male should be adequate unless pollinating large crops. Other branches may be stripped of flowers to help contain pollen and guard against accidental, random pollination. Isolate the male from the females once flowers begin to develop by placing him in a sunny window or on the perimeter of a vegetative grow room. Decreased light makes pollen sacks develop more slowly.

Cut a branch of ripe male flowers and place it in a glass of water, just like a spray of cut flowers. It will remain healthy for several weeks if water is changed daily. When the pollen sacks open, proceed with step three. The remaining male plant may then be cut back or harvested.

Step Three: When pollen pods start to open, place a clean, French bread sack or baggie over the branch to collect pollen. Secure the bag at the bottom with a piece of string or wire tie. Keep the bag over the branch for several days to collect pollen.

Step Four: When enough pollen has been collected, shake remaining pollen into the bag and remove spent branch.

Step Five: Ideally, pistils should be ready for fertilization 3 to 4 weeks after the first calyx has appeared. Receptive pistils are white and fuzzy. Cover the selected female branch that has many unfertilized white receptive pistils with the pollen filled bag. To pollinate the entire branch, shake the bag.

Step Six: Use a small artist's paint brush to apply the pollen from the bag to selected pistils if you want a few seeds. Be very careful. Use a little pollen on each set of pistils and keep it from spreading to the *sinsemilla* crop.

Step Seven: Leave the bag on the female for a day or longer to ensure the entire branch is fertilized. Be careful not to scatter pollen on adjacent *sinsemilla* crop when removing the bag.

Step Eight: After fertilization, seeds will be ripe in 3 - 6 weeks. Harvest seeds when they split open the containing calyx or rattle in the pod.

Step Nine: Let seeds dry for 2 - 3 months, in a cool, dry place, before planting.

Seed Crops

Seed crops are mature when the seeds are a rich dark brown. Often ripe seeds split open their containing seed bract. THC content is usually of minimum importance, but seeded buds still pack a whollop. Seeded branches are ready about a week after *sinsemilla* crops. Seed crops can be left in the ground until seeds actually rattle in the pod.

If one or two branches are pollinated on a female, the remaining unpollinated branches are *sinsemilla*. Harvest *sinsemilla* crop when ripe and let seeded flowers stay in the ground until seeds are clearly mature.

Remove mature seeds from pods and store them in a cool, dry place. Seeds are viable as soon as they are harvested, but may germinate poorly. Seeds that dry out a few weeks after harvest develop a hard shell and germinate much better.

How Cannabis Grows

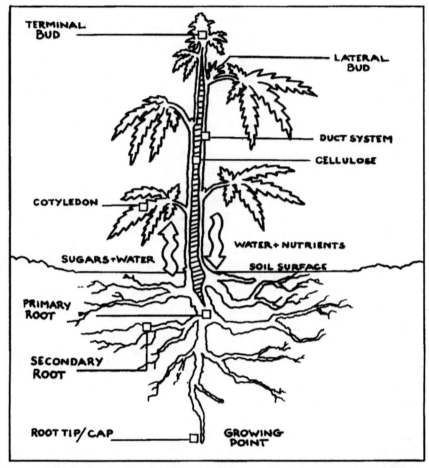

All plants produce food by combining mineral nutrients, chemicals captured from the air and sunshine combined with water and a growing medium.

Marijuana is an annual plant which completes its life cycle in a single year. A seed planted in the spring will grow bushy and tall through the summer and flower in the fall, producing more seeds. The cycle starts over again the next year.

The seed has an outside coating, which protects the plant's embryo and a supply of stored food within. With heat, moisture and air a healthy seed will germinate and grow. The seeds coating splits, a rootlet grows downward, and a sprout with seed leaves pushes upwards in search of light.

The single root from the seed grows down and branches out, similar to the way the stem branches out above ground. Tiny rootlets draw in water and nutrients (chemical substances needed for life). Roots anchor a plant in the ground. As the plant matures, the roots take on specialized functions. The center contains a water transport system and may also store food. The tips of the roots grow into the soil to find water and food. The single-celled *root hairs* are the parts of the root that actually absorb water and nutrients. Without water, these frail root hairs will dry up and die. They are very delicate and are easily damaged by light, air, or clumsy hands when moved or exposed. Because of this, extreme care must be exercised during transplanting.

As the stem grows upwards it also produces new buds along the sides. The central bud carries growth upward and side or lateral buds turn into branches or leaves. The stem transmits water and nutrients from the delicate root hairs to the growing buds, leaves and flowers.

Sugars and starches, manufactured in the leaves, are distributed through the plant via the stem. This fluid flow takes place near the surface of the stem. If the stem is bound too tightly by string or other tie downs, the flow of life giving fluids, strangling and eventually killing the plant. The stem also supports the plant with stiff cellulose, located within the inner walls. Outdoors, rain and wind push a plant around, causing much stiff cellulose production to keep the plant supported upright.

Cannabis will flower if conditions are right, the main variable is the photoperiod (the length of daylight and darkness). In the fall, the days become shorter and plants are signaled that the annual life cycle is coming to an end. The plant's functions change. Leafy growth slows and flowers start to form.

Cannabis has both male and female plants. When both female and male flowers are in bloom, pollen from the male flower lands on the female flower, thereby fertilizing it. The male dies after producing and shedding as much pollen as possible. Seeds form and grow within the female flowers. THC-rich resin (see Sinsemilla Harvest in Chapter Four) production slows and soon stops. As the seeds are maturing, the female plant slowly dies. The mature seeds then fall to the ground and germinate naturally or are collected for planting.

The female *Cannabis* flower, left unfertilized is called sin-semilla, Spanish for "without seed". The female continues to produce larger flowers and more resins while waiting for male pollen. After several weeks of heavy flower and resin production, THC production peaks out. This is the perfect time to pick the ripe, resin coated buds.

When planted in the earth, *Cannabis* roots branch out and penetrate deep into the soil in search of water and nutrients. *Cannabis* tends to grow above ground at the same rate as it grows below the soil's surface. If root growth is inhibited because of an inability to find water and nutrients, growth slows to a crawl. Lateral branches spread out about as far as the plants roots are able to spread out. It is super important to remember how much root space *cannabis* needs and to provide enough fertile soil to meet those needs. If roots must be in a pot or planter box, the restriction requires them to have perfect soil and extra care.

The Cannabinoids

Cannabis is the only plant known to contain cannabinoids, chemical substances that are psychoactive. Of more than 35 different cannabinoids, the three most important are THC, CBD and CBN.

THC (tetrahydrocannabinol – delta 9) is the main mind-altering ingredient in *Cannabis* . Scholars calculate that 70 to 100 percent of the high is derived from THC. Virtually all *cannabis* contains THC and concentrations range from traces to more than 95 percent of all cannabinoids. The most potent *cannabis* buds (dried, manicured flower tops) can have up to 25 percent THC by dry weight.

CBD (cannabidiol) is also found in practically all *cannabis* in a range of densities of less than one percent to more than 95 percent of all cannabinoids. Alone, CBD is not mind-bending, but combined with THC it interacts to make the high more sedate, last longer or delay the onset.

CBN (cannabinol) is produced as THC and is broken down or degraded (oxidized) into CBN. CBN is seldom present in fresh marijuana. Poor curing and storage practices that expose buds to air, light and friction encourage development of CBN.

For a complete discussion of cannabinoids, see *Marijuana Grower's Guide*, by Mel Frank, Redeye Press, 1997.

Soil

Air, water, minerals and organic matter are the most important non-living elements of soil. Spaces between soil particles are conduits for air and water. Plenty of space must be available in soil for air and water to move in*. Minerals used in gardening must first be changed, by a slightly acidic water solution and bacteria and other soil life, into food for plants.

*That's why good soil is described as "fluffy" by some growers.

Humus – organic matter – is the binding fiber. It is as important to the soil as dietary fiber is to the human body. Humus keeps the soil loose and spongy allowing movement of air and water and holds nutrients and moisture for roots to absorb.

Organic matter fuels the bacteria in soil. Heat, air and water are also needed for these bacteria to act, and all are promoted by good soil structure and texture. When the soil warms in the spring, the bacterial activity increases. It is through their activity that nutrients are changed into compounds that can be absorbed by plants.

To get the feel of your soil's texture, scoop up a handful of moist soil and rub it through your fingers. Clay soil feels and looks slippery. Sandy soil feels and looks gritty. Silty loam, which is in between clay and sand, almost feels greasy, but is less slippery than clay. The majority of soils are a combination of clay and sand. Loam is the combination of humus, sand and clay.

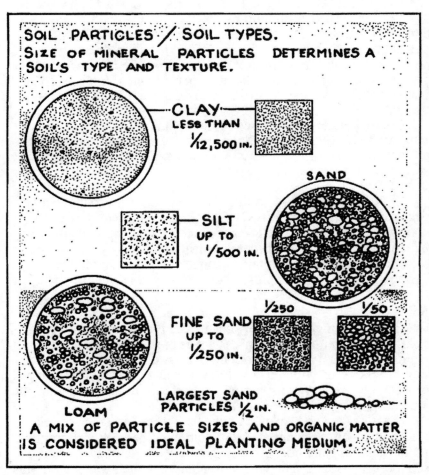

Fine clay particles are very small and allow very slow drainage. Silt offers a perfect water retention and drainage. Fine sand particles are large, allowing fast drainage.

Clay Soils

Clay soil, also called "adobe" or "heavy soil", consists of fine to medium particles packed tightly together. About 100 particles of fine clay soil would fit into this period (.). Clay soil is very dense and weighs more than sandy or loamy soils. This soil holds water well, but leaves little room for air, and thus inhibits root growth. The finer the mineral particles, the heavier the clay and the slower the drainage.

Clay soils are found along coastal areas and also very common among inland soils.

Heavy clay soils are difficult to work when wet, sticking to tools and clumping into rock-hard clods when dry. Heavily compacted clay soil is found worldwide. Clay soils are also slow to warm in the spring, but can hold warmth into the fall.

Clay soils hold fertilizers well but tend to be acidic. Organic matter, such as compost and leaf mold when added to clay soils, make millions of tiny air pockets, improve drainage and promote root growth. Perfecting the structure of heavy clay soil can take several years. A large planting hole filled with well-rotted compost and potting soil will have the best structure.

Contrary to popular belief, adding small amounts of sand, unless special sharp river sand is used, to clay soil does not promote better drainage; it binds with clay to form a cement-like product.

Digging big yard square planting holes and adding much organic matter and good soil is the quickest way to improve heavy clay soils.

Sandy Soils

The recommendation of small medium and large particles in sand allow excellent root penetration and air space. Light, sandy soils are generally easy to till even when saturated with water. Sandy soils warm quickly in the spring and produce early crops. Sandy soils do not hold fertilizers well, particularly when over-watered.

Sandy soils are found near oceans, in deserts and in many inland regions around the world.

Compost, blended with sandy soil, binds the large particles together so that they hold water. The compost is soon "eaten" by bacteria and other soil organisms. Organic matter decomposes rapidly in hot climates. The more often the soil is cultivated and the more organic matter added, the better.

Mulch, spread on top of sandy soil, keeps it cooler and reduces evaporation. Winter cover crops are essential to hold moisture, prevent runoff, and retain life in the soil. Compost and peat moss are some of the best materials to use to improve sandy soils.

What kind of Soil do you have?

What do the following tests show you?

Check soil texture by picking up a handful of moist (not soggy) soil and gently squeezing it.

The ideal loam soil, will barely stay together when pressed. When you slowly open up your hand to release pressure it will fall apart. Do you have loamy soil?

Sandy soil feels gritty and falls apart readily with little or no humus to bind it together. Do you have sandy soil?

Clay soil will stay in a ball. The finer the clay, the tighter the ball of soil when you squeeze it. Very heavy clay soil feels slick and slimy. Do you have clay soil?

If your soil is predominantly clay or sand, use the soil amendments mentioned above to improve fertility, tilth and drainage or water holding ability.

If your soil is clay, dig a big planting hole at least one yard square (the bigger the better) and amend the hole with compost, (potting) soil, good top soil and organic nutrients. Raise the bed on top of the planting hole to improve drainage, and add a handful of dolomite lime per cubic foot of soil.

Make the shape of the hole very large on the surface, such as two square yards. Dig down about 8 inches for 2 square yards. Then, slope the hole to the bottom of one square yard. This way the roots will be able to find lots of food and moisture, just like in nature. Most of the roots tend to grow down 2 - 4 inches in the soil. Deeper roots will extract non-soluble nutrients and moisture. The roots near the surface of the soil stabilize the plant, provide moisture and supply much of the food the plant receives.

If your soil is sandy, dig a big hole and place boards at the bottom of the hole to stop downward water flow, add compost, good soil, organic nutrients, polymers (special water-holding crystals that keep water and release it over time into the drying soil), and dolomite lime. Compost, polymers and the board at the bottom of the hole will hold more water. Make the top of the hole a bit concave to catch any moisture or rainwater.

Loam Soils

Dark, fertile loam soils are ideal for growing marijuana. They are easy to work and hold air and nutrients well. Coarse loamy soil contains large soil particles which hold air and allow root growth, plus enough clay to retain moisture. Fine loamy soils contain more clay with less sand. Loam soils are fertile.

Loam soils are found in ancient river bottoms and lake beds, where sedimentary soil built up. Loam is the ideal concentration of sand, clay and organic matter, combining the advantages of clay (moisture retention and fertilizer retention) and sand (quickly warming, good drainage, and easy to work).

pH

pH is a scale from 1.0 to 14.0 that measures the acid-to-alkaline balance. One (1.0) is the most acidic, 7.0 is neutral, and 14.0 is most alkaline. The pH scale is a logarithmic scale. For example, a soil with a pH of 8.0 is 10 times more alkaline than a soil with a pH of 7.5. A soil with a pH of 5.5 is 10 times more acid than a soil with a pH of 6.5.

The pH of a soil is one of many conditions that affect plant growth. Clay soils are usually acid (pH below 7) and many sandy soils are alkaline (pH above 7). Marijuana grows best in a slightly acidic soil with a pH between 6.0 and 6.8. Within this range roots can absorb and process available nutrients. If the pH is too low (acidic), manganese can concentrate to toxic levels and calcium, phosphorus and magnesium availability is limited. In an alkaline soil – with a pH above 7.0 – phosphorus, iron, copper, zinc, boron and manganese availability is limited.

There are several ways to measure *p*H. A *p*H soil test kit, litmus paper, or electronic *p*H tester the last of which is easiest to use. When testing for *p*H, take two or three soil samples and follow the manufacturer's instructions carefully.

Lime raises the *p*H, sulfur lowers the *p*H.

```
pH
4.  4.5  5.0  5.5  6.0  6.5  7.0  7.5  8.0  8.5  9

                    NITROGEN

                  PHOSPHORUS

                  POTASSIUM

                    SULFUR

                   CALCIUM

                  MAGNESIUM

           IRON

        MANGANESE

          BORON

       COPPER / ZINC

                  MOLYBDENUM
```

Water and soil pH are exceptionally important. The ideal pH range for nutrient uptake is 6 – 6.8. When the pH is above 7.5 or below 5.5, nutrient uptake becomes a very big problem.

Soil *p*H is easy to change. Adding some form of lime to acid soil will increase the *p*H, lessening acidity. Adding too much lime will make some nutrients unavailable or burn plant roots. See below for approximate amounts of lime to alter soil *p*H. Check with local farmers, nurseries or government agricultural agencies for recommendations on applying lime to your soil if the *p*H needs more than one full point of adjustment.

Approximate lime application rates for different soils
35 pounds/300 square yards very sandy soil
50 pounds/300 square yards sandy soil
70 pounds/300 square yards loam
80 pounds/300 square yards heavy clay soil

Types of Lime

Agricultural or ground limestone (calcium carbonate) is one of the most common forms of lime and an excellent choice. It is slow acting and will remain in the soil for several years.

Dolomite lime (calcium magnesium carbonate) combines calcium with magnesium to formulate an excellent *pH* -altering substance, and adds two much-used nutrients as well. Always buy slow-acting dolomite flour in the smallest particle size available, this helps it begin acting soon after application. Even the finest grade will remain in the soil for up to five years.

Ground oyster shells contain calcium carbonate and small amounts of phosphorus. Oyster shells, sold as "chicken scratch", are commonly available at feed stores. Oyster shells are very slow to decompose.

Hydrated lime (calcium hydroxide) is quick acting and caustic to plants and microorganisms. (Not recommended)

Quicklime (calcium oxide), manufactured by searing or burning limestone, is fast acting, but caustic, and may burn or kill plants and soil microorganisms. (Not recommended)

Wood ashes are a source of lime, as well as phosphorus, potassium (potash), boron and other elements. Hardwood ashes are about twice as alkaline as softwood ashes. Wood ashes are soluble and wash out of the soil quickly. Not a good choice to alter *pH*.

For best results, use the finest grind of dolomite lime (flour), and apply it in the fall so that it will affect the *pH* by following spring. Do not apply lime to a freshly manured soil, or it will combine to form ammonia gas, which will release needed nitrogen into the air.

It is possible to lower the *pH* by adding liberal amounts of compost, peat, or acidic organic matter, such as coffee grounds or citrus waste, to the soil. If a soil has a *pH* over 8.0, build a raised bed on top of the soil at least 12 inches high, so that the alkaline salts and water stay below the level of most feeder roots. If you can see white alkaline salts on the surface of the soil, water very, very heavily and add gypsum (80 pounds per 100 square feet) to leach the alkaline salts deeper into the soil. This practice may have to be repeated every spring.

The most common element used to lower the *pH* is sulfur. Safe-to-use compounds include iron sulfate and magnesium sulfate. Avoid marijuana-toxic aluminum sulfate. However, if any sulfur compound is added in large quantities, toxic levels result. Adding gypsum to soils with a *pH* of 7.5 will free sulfur compounds and lower *pH*. If *pH* is above 7.5, add gypsum to free sulfur salts and test *pH* before adding sulfur. Local nursery or county extension services can provide more specific guidelines on lowering the *pH* of alkaline soil. Also see "Gypsum" in the "Organic Fertilizers" section.

To lower the pH use sulfur.

Approximate sulfur application rates to lower pH to 7.0
If pH is 7.5 add 5 pounds per 1000 square feet
If pH is 8.0 add 25 pounds per 1000 square feet
If pH is 8.5 add 35 pounds per 1000 square feet

Potting soil is the easiest choice for container cultivation. It is usually pH balanced, contains adequate levels of most all nutrients, retains water and air evenly, drains well, and allows easy root growth. Most potting soils will be depleted of nutrients within 3 – 4 weeks. After this time, supplemental fertilization will usually be necessary. Check the pH before using.

Soil Amendments

Soil amendments are the things added to increase the soils air and water retaining ability. Amendments are either mineral or organic.

Mineral amendments are near neutral on the pH scale, and contain virtually no nutrients of their own. They decompose through weathering and erosion, which does not affect soil pH. The amendments are also very lightweight, making them easy to pack to remote areas.

Perlite holds water and nutrients well, and aerates the soil. It drains fast and does not promote salt build-up. Medium and coarse grades of perlite are the best choice.

Pumice (volcanic rock) is very light, and holds water, nutrients and air in its many catacomb-like holes. It is a good amendment for aerating the soil and retaining moisture evenly.

Vermiculite holds much water, nutrients and air within its fiber, and gives body to fast draining soils. Vermiculite is available in fine, medium and coarse grades. Use the fine as a rooting medium for clones/cuttings and the coarse grade as an amendment to heavy soil.

Organic soil amendments break down through bacterial activity, slowly yielding humus as an end product. Humus is a soft, spongy material that binds minute soil particles together, improving the soil texture. Young, composting organic soil amendments require nitrogen to carry on their bacterial decomposition. If they do not contain at least 1.5 percent nitrogen, the organic amendment will get it from the soil, robbing roots of nitrogen. When using organic amendments, make sure they are thoroughly composted (at least one year) and releasing nitrogen rather than taking it from the soil. A good sign of fertility is a dark, rich color.

There are many kinds of manure: cow manure, horse manure, rabbit manure, chicken manure, and the less common pig and duck manure. Their nutrient content varies. Manures are all a source of nitrogen. See below.

Peat moss is the term used to describe partially decomposed vegetation; the decaying process has been slowed by the wet and cold conditions of the northern marsh lands. Once dry, it can be difficult to re-wet.

To combine soil amendments, dry-mix all of the components, then water the mix adding a wetting agent like liquid concentrate soap (2 - 3 drops per gallon).

Soilless Mix

Soilless mix, an alternative to soil, is generally made from one or all of the following: pumice, vermiculite, perlite, sand, and peat moss. Soilless mix is my favorite. It allows for good, even root growth, and it's inexpensive.

Soilless mix has good texture, contains no nutrients of its own, unless fortified with nutrients, and is generally at or near 7 on the pH scale. It drains fairly rapidly, may be leached efficiently, and there is little build up of nutrients to toxic levels. Commercial soilless mixes are fortified with small amounts of all necessary nutrients. The fortified nutrients last for about a month. It is a good idea to use a fertilizer containing trace elements. After that, supplemental fertilization will be necessary to sustain vigorous growth.

RULE OF THUMB: Mix soilless amendments outdoors and when they are dry. Use a respirator to avoid inhaling dust.

Containers

All shapes and sizes of containers are available and they can be constructed of almost anything. Any container that is clean and has never been used to hold any petroleum products is OK. Clay pots are a poor choice. They are heavy and absorb moisture from soil inside, causing soil to dry out quickly. Wood pots and planters are easy to construct and offer some insulation from the sun if the sides are thick. Plastic containers are also a good choice. Grow bags, 8 – 12-mill-thick, are a good, inexpensive, long lasting alternative to rigid containers. Some people use the sack the potting soil came in as a container. Once the soil is inside and moist, the bag holds its shape well. The bags tend to expand and contract with the soil, lessening the chance of burned root tips that grow down the side of the pot. However, do take care not to disrupt growth by disturbing the root ball, if moving grow bags. Styrofoam containers are an excellent alternative.

Drainage holes in the bottom of all containers are essential. They should let the excess water drain easily, but not be so big that soil in the bottom of the container washes away. Lining pots with newspaper will slow fast drainage and keep soil contained.

RULE OF THUMB: have a minimum of two ½-inch holes per square foot of bottom. When using a tray under pot, do not let excess water sit in the tray for more than 3 days. This stagnant water could cause root rot and fungus.

Use gravel or large rocks – up to two or three inches – in the bottom of a pot to slow drainage on sunny terrace gardens. The difference between the size of the gravel and the particles of soil create pressure that holds the water and keeps it from draining.

The size of container is very important. *Cannabis* grows very rapidly, requiring a lot of root space for vigorous growth. If the roots are confined, plant growth slows to a crawl.

Marijuana roots develop quickly. When roots reach the sides of the pot, they grow down and circle the inside of the pot. When the sun heats pots, the soil contracts and pulls away from the container wall. When this happens, the root hairs die and no longer absorb water and nutrients. To prevent this contraction problem, run your finger around the inside lip of the pot, cultivating the soil, filling the crack between the pot and soil. Maintain evenly moist soil to help keep root hairs on the soil perimeter from drying out. Transplant before the plant is pot bound and stunted. Once a plant is stunted, it will take several weeks to grow enough new roots and root hairs to resume normal growth.

The best way to keep plants easy-to-maintain is to plant seedlings or clones directly into a 5- or 10-gallon pot. This method requires fewer containers, less work and is less stressful to plants. Many growers plant several clones/seedlings per container and weed out the weakest plants, leaving one or two strong plants.

RULE OF THUMB: allow 2 gallons of soil for every month the plant will spend in the container. A 10 gallon pot will support a seedling or clone for more than 6 months.

Containers that sit in the sun get hot – very hot! A black container sitting in bright sunshine can reach temperatures in excess of 120 degrees F. in less than an hour. The majority of feeder roots are located around the perimeter of the container, next to the container's wall. Fragile hair-like feeder roots cook in a few minutes at temperatures above 100 degrees F. Dead feeder roots cannot supply water and nutrients to a plant. The plant is stunted until more feeder roots grow. No amount of water or fertilizer can bring the dead roots back to life.

Solve the hot pot dilemma by placing the growing pot inside

another pot to deflect the hot sunshine. This simple insulating layer will create a cool air space between the two pots. Or you could make a sun shield to deflect the sun and keep the container cool. This simple cooling technique could double harvest volume.

If possible, use white containers that reflect heat rather than absorb heat when planting in warm areas. Dark containers can also be used to collect heat for an early crop in the spring. White containers can still get very hot and must be shaded.

Baked clay ceramic tiles and concrete on terraces and balconies hold the heat during the day, and cool to below air temperature at night. To keep container temperatures steady, raise the pot off the hot/cold floor to allow air to circulate below. A mulch of white rocks, plastic, shells, etc. placed on the soil surface around the plant helps to retain moisture while deflecting heat.

Water

Rivers and creeks originating from rainwater and springs are most often clean sources of irrigation water. Polluted urban rivers carrying toxic chemical fertilizer runoff should be avoided. If drawing irrigation water from the river, always use flowing water rather than stagnant pools.

TRENCH CHANNELS RAINWATER.

Small trenches direct runoff water to individual plants.

Well water that tastes good is normally OK to use for growing. Check the *p*H of the water, as well as the dissolved salts content. This information is normally on file at the county water quality department. Many times the *p*H is out of the acceptable 6.0 to 6.8 range. Desert regions are prone to have alkaline water with a *p*H above 7.0 and many high rainfall areas have a *p*H below 6.0.

Water containing sulfur is easily smelled and tasted. Saline water is more difficult to detect. Salts from saline water (common in coastal and desert areas) or fertilizer residue can quickly build up to toxic levels in container gardens, salts present less of a problem in soil gardens. Excessive salts inhibit seed germination, burn the root hairs and tips or edges of leaves, and stunt the plant. Excess salt built up in the soil can be leached out by pouring at least 2 gallons of water per gallon of growing medium. Repeat leaching once or twice

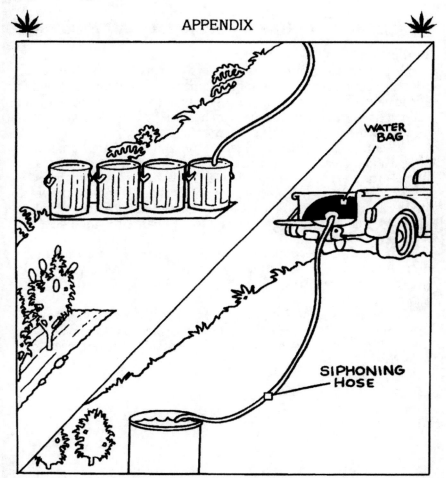

Growers store siphoned water for a month or longer.

if burn is severe.

Reservoirs come in all shapes and sizes. Fifty-gallon plastic garbage cans nest inside of one another, are inexpensive, easy-to-hide, and lightweight. Green and brown reservoirs (the preferred colors) are used to store runoff rainwater or water that is pumped or siphoned into them. Keep the lids fastened down to avoid evaporation and small rodents enter.

Large collapsible plastic tanks are also available through farm supply outlets. Similar to a waterbed, these reservoirs are fitted into a hole in the ground or stored above ground. Some growers make their own reservoir. They dig a hole 3 – 4 feet wide and 3 – 4 feet deep and as long as necessary, before lining the hole with a waterproof plastic tarp. They cover and camouflage the tarp with nearby debris.

Application

Large plants use much more water than small plants. The age of the plant, container size, soil type, temperature, humidity and wind all contribute to water needs. Change any one of these variables and water consumption will change. The healthier a plant, the faster it grows and the more water it consumes.

Water early in the day so excess water will evaporate from soil surface and leaves. Leaving foliage and soil wet at night promotes fungus attack especially during flowering in more humid climates.

Some gardeners irrigate gardens on a wet and dry cycle. They let soil dry out to about two inches below the soil surface before the next watering. Container gardens are watered after the top one inch of the soil is dried out.

Other growers keep moisture more consistent by irrigating more often. A mild fertilizer solution is often added with each watering. If unable to water regularly, make sure soil holds enough water between waterings.

Cannabis does not like soggy soil. Soil kept too wet drowns roots, making it impossible for them to breathe, resulting in slow growth. Tiny root hairs dry up and die if the soil dries out, even in pockets.

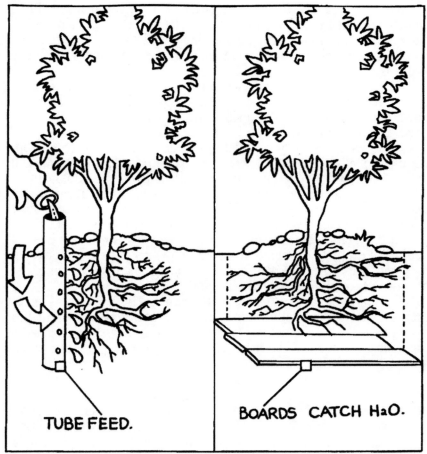

TUBE FEED.

BOARDS CATCH H₂O.

Water sinks deeply into soil with the aid of a plastic pipe with holes drilled in the side. Boards, large rocks or plastic buried in a planting hole catches water, lowers water needs.

Flowering marijuana consumes large amounts of water to carry on rapid floral formation. Letting a flowering plant wilt between waterings actually stunts flower formation. If unable to irrigate regularly, make sure all drought measures are in place.

Overwatering can be a special problem with small plants. Remember, too much water drowns roots by cutting off their supply of oxygen and small plants are most susceptible. Sometimes, parts of the soil are overwatered and other soil pockets remain bone dry. Cultivating the soil surface and allowing even water penetration will overcome this problem. Signs of overwatering are: leaves curl and yellow, soggy soil, fungus, and slow growth.

RULES OF THUMB about irrigation: 1. Irrigate small seedlings and clones when the soil surface is dry. The surface is dry almost daily on rooting clones with good drainage and no humidity tent. 2. Irrigate larger plants in the vegetative and flowering stages when soil is dry 1-2" below the surface.

Cultivating the soil surface allows water to penetrate evenly and guards against dry soil pockets. It also keeps water from running down the crack between the inside of the pot and the soil. Gently break up and cultivate the top ½-inch of soil.

If the soil is nearly or completely dry, add a few drops (one drop per pint) of a biodegradable, concentrated liquid soap to the water. It will help the water penetrate soil more efficiently and guard against dry soil pockets. Apply about ¼ to ½ as much water/fertilizer as the plant is expected to need, wait 10 to 15 minutes for it to totally soak in, then apply more water/fertilizer until the soil is evenly moist.

Drip irrigation cuts water use by 30 to 50 percent. Water is applied in droplets through a network of low-pressure tubing over a long period of time. The water soaks into each plant's root zone slowly. Evaporation is virtually eliminated.

A drip system cuts watering maintenance. These systems use low pressure plastic pipe with friction fittings. Water flows down the pipe and out the emitters, one drop at a time. The emitters are attached to the main hose and may be either spaghetti tube or nipple type. There are many drip irrigation kits and components on the market.

Chances are good that you will have to siphon, pump or pack water to the remote garden. If siphoning, allow for the greatest incline possible. The incline and a large diameter hose ensure the water will move quickly and debris will be washed through the hose.

To make a siphon or gravity fed watering system, place a barrel at least 3 feet above (uphill) from garden. Place a siphon hose in the top of the tank or install a PVC on/off valve near the bottom of the barrel. A float valve may also be installed in the barrel so there is a constant supply of water.

Gasoline powered pumps are the best alternative for many growers. Gasoline is a lightweight, inexpensive, portable fuel. When buying the pump, make sure it is adequate for the job. A visit to a pump supply store will be enlightening. Pretend you are buying a pump for an application on a farm to water animals or irrigate from a pond. Make a drawing of the pumping situation before going to buy the pump and include all the pertinent data, such as how much water you want to move, how far you want to move it, and how many feet you want to lift it.

Much rainwater can be collected from rooftops during rainy season. Catching water is inconspicuous with a large green or brown tarp that blends into the countryside. Catch-water drains into a large holding tank. Tanks are easy to hide and will last for many years if protected from sunlight.

Some growers fill containers with water and truck it to their garden regularly. They park above the patch and gravity flow water down to the garden with a hose.

Dry polymer crystals, about the size of rock salt, expand to more than 10 times their size when wet. They hold water within the soil and release it slowly over time. Add polymer crystals to the planting hole or containers when preparing. Make sure to mix polymers evenly with soil so they do not stratify or bunch up.

RULE OF THUMB - Water early in the day so excess water will evaporate from soil surface and leaves. Leaving foliage and soil wet at night promotes fungus attack.

Bury a 2 – 3-inch pipe alongside the planting hole with several small holes along the side. Fill the pipe with water to irrigate. The water will trickle out the holes into the soil and little will be lost to evaporation.

Other simple ways to save irrigation water include these:

Moisture evaporation is slowed dramatically by a protective layer of mulch on the soil's surface. Water soon evaporates from the surface of unmulched soil, but is retained much longer when a thick, wide layer of mulch (6 inches x 3 feet) is used. Mulch also prevents rapid temperature fluctuations. Although the sun bakes the surface of bare soil, increasing the temperature significantly, the surface temperature of soil protected with mulch changes very little. This buffering of the ambient temperature protects feeder roots near the surface. To achieve warmer temperatures for germination in cool spring weather, just pull the protective mulch aside so the sun can warm the soil. After the seedlings grow a few inches tall, brush the mulch back around them.

Organic mulch, such as straw, leaves, wood chips, grass, weeds, brush, etc., are the best choices when available. Plastic, stone, shells, etc., also function as mulch. For more information on mulch see: The Ruth Stout No-Work Garden Book, Rodale Press, 1971.

In fast-draining soil, place large flat rocks in the bottom of the planting hole to impair the flow of water. Both wood and paper will use valuable nitrogen in the soil to decompose and are not advised.

Fertilizers
Nutrients and Fertilizers

    Cannabis grows so fast that most soils cannot supply all necessary nutrients for rapid, healthy growth. Fertilizing is necessary to make extra nutrients available for sustained, vigorous growth.

    The goal of fertilizing is to supply the plant with proper amounts of nutrients for vigorous growth without toxifying the soil by over-fertilizing. A 5 - 6 gallon container or a 3-foot square planting hole

Macronutrinets are listed on fertilizer packages, usually in three big numbers that stand for nitrogen (N), phosphorus (P), and potassium (K). For example the NPK of one super bloom fertilizer is 5-50-17.

full of rich, fertile soil will supply all the necessary nutrients for a month or longer After the roots have absorbed most of the initially available N-P-K nutrients, more of the nutrients must be added to the soil to sustain vigorous growth. Normally nitrogen is the first nutrient to become deficient.

A *cannabis* plant has differing fertilizer needs as it grows older. During germination and seedling growth, intake of phosphorus is high. The vegetative growth stage requires high amounts of nitrogen for green leafy growth. Phosphorus and potassium are also necessary in substantial levels; a general purpose N-P-K fertilizer is recommended. In the flowering stage, phosphorus intake is highest and nitrogen and potassium are less important. Using a super bloom fertilizer low in nitrogen and potassium and high in phosphorus promotes larger flower growth. A high nitrogen content fertilizer promotes greener, leafy growth during flowering. *Cannabis* needs some nitrogen during flowering. Without nitrogen, older foliage yellows and dies prematurely.

Fertilizers are either (water) soluble or gradual release. Both soluble and gradual release fertilizers can be organic or chemical.

Soluble fertilizers (chemical or organic) are preferred by many guerilla growers. Soluble fertilizers dissolve in water and may be added or washed (leached) out of the soil easily. It is easy to control the exact amount of nutrients available to plants in a soluble form. Soluble fertilizer may be applied in a water solution to the soil or misted directly on the leaves.

Chemical granular fertilizers can easily be over applied, be careful! They are difficult to leach out fast enough to save the plant.

Osmocote™ is a time release chemical fertilizer that is easy to apply and only requires one application every few months. This type of fertilizer is convenient for guerilla growers with remote gardens that are difficult to access.

Vitamin B[1]

Vitamin B[1] helps roots absorb moisture better when disturbed during transplanting. Vitamin B[1] is highly recommended when transplanting seedlings or cuttings under adverse guerilla growing conditions. Smart growers use Vitamin B[1] any time they transplant.

Applying Fertilizer

Organic mixes in large planting holes normally need a high nitrogen fertilizer that is applied several times through the vegetative growing stage. Remember, plants in small containers use available nutrients quickly and need frequent fertilizing, while plants in the earth, or large planters have more soil to supply more nutrients, and require less frequent fertilizing.

Look at your garden. If plants are growing well with green healthy leaves, they are probably getting all necessary nutrients from the soil. The moment growth slows, or leaves begin to turn pale green, it is time to fertilize.

I like to experiment on two or three test plants to develop my horticultural skills. Clones work especially well for this type of experiment. Give the test plants some fertilizer and see if they green up and grow faster. If it is good for one, it should be good for all.

How much fertilizer? Each plant will answer this question. Just mix fertilizer as per instructions and water as normal, or dilute fertilizer and apply more often. Remember, small plants use much less fertilizer than large ones. Fertilize early in the day, so plants have all day to absorb and process the fertilizer.

General rules for fertilizer use:

Follow directions on fertilizer package. Apply a complete N-P-K fertilizer 7 - 10 days before planting. Apply a high-nitrogen supplemental fertilizer to stimulate leaf growth every 2 - 4 weeks during peak growing season in the summer. Apply a fertilizer high in phosphorus to increase bud development. Apply a biweekly dilute liquid fertilizer to plants in containers.

Foliar Feeding

Foliar feeding (misting the leaves with fertilizer solution) makes some nutrients available and usable immediately. Food is absorbed directly into the leaves. Foliar feeding is a good way to keep toxic nutrient levels from building up in the soil, but like soil fertilization, may be over done. Daily foliar feeding with a weak solution leaches the nutrients from the leaves, just as excessive watering leaches nutrients from the soil. A good foliar feeding program would start after the plant's first month of growth. Apply fertilizer solution with a fine spray.

Foliar feeding is more work and creates fast results. Nitrogen deficient plants can turn from pale yellow to lime green in 24-48 hours! The nutrients are supplied directly and used immediately. Soil condition or *p*H are not affected, but root absorption may improve. A combination of soil and foliar feeding is common. Good organic foliar fertilizers are fish emulsion, bat guano and kelp. Of course, the tea must be strained through a filter of several layers of cheese cloth to prevent the sprayer from clogging.

Fertilizer Elements

There are many different elements, called nutrients, that are essential for plant life. Carbon, hydrogen and oxygen are absorbed from the air and water. The rest of the nutrients are absorbed mainly from the soil. The primary, or macro-nutrients, nitrogen (N), phosphorus (P), and potassium (K), are the elements a plant uses the most. Fertilizers show the N-P-K percentages in big numbers on

Incorporate well-rotted manures and organic matter when cultivating beds. When sowing seed, or transplanting seedlings, dig the hole several inches deeper than necessary, add a handful of a complete fertilizer mix, then cover it with soil before inserting the seed or transplant. Do not side dress seeds or new transplants with fertilizer or the roots will tend to stay on the surface or grow upward toward the fertilizer. If growth slows later in the season, apply a side dressing or liquid fertilizer. Regular applications of soluble teas will keep plants growing well. Foliar feeding, spraying dilute soluble fertilizer directly on leaves, makes nutrients immediately available. A high-nitrogen soluble fertilizer, such as fish emulsion, will green-up a tired garden. A dilute liquid seaweed application can solve most trace element deficiency problems. If this remedy fails to cure the problem, seek professional advice. Use a siphon mixer or small spray bottle to apply soluble teas. Most organic fertilizers must be spaded into the soil before becoming available to plants.

the front of the package. Secondary nutrients include calcium and magnesium and are also used in fair quantities. The remaining nutrients, called trace elements, are necessary in minute amounts. A complete fertilizer contains all of the primary and secondary nutrients, plus a full range of necessary trace elements.

Nitrogen (N) is the most important nutrient. Nitrogen is essential to the production of chlorophyll leaf and stem growth as well as overall size and vigor. Nitrogen is most active in young buds, shoots and leaves. Marijuana loves nitrogen and requires high levels during vegetative growth.

Most forms of nitrogen are water soluble and quickly washed or leached from the soil. Consequently, nitrogen is required often.

Nitrogen is the most common nutrient found deficient. Nitrogen deficiency causes growth to be stunted and old leaves to develop smaller and turn yellow. Remedy by fertilizing with N or N-P-K fertilizer. For fast results, foliar feed.

Excess nitrogen causes plants to grow too fast. Stems become spindly and the leaves lush green. But the plant tissue is soft, weak and more susceptible to damage from insects, disease, drought, heat and cold.

Foliar feeding, spraying plants with pH neutral fertilizer water, delivers nutrients to plants immediately, regardless of soil chemistry. Irrigating with soluble fertilizer is still subject to soil pH and chemistry.

Phosphorus (P) is associated with overall vigor, flower, and seed production. *Cannabis* uses highest levels during germination, seedling and flower growth. Decomposition of organic matter and the effects of changing heat and moisture level in the soil release phosphorus and other elements into the soil.

Phosphorus deficiency is not common. A lack of phosphorus is often confused with a nitrogen deficiency because both have many of the same symptoms. However, phosphorus-deficient plants have dull, deep green leaves, and often the stems will turn shades of purple. Overall growth is slow, maturity is delayed and flower development is retarded. It is uncommon for phosphorus to leach out of the soil. If soluble fertilizer is over-applied, you should be able to leach it out of the soil.

Excess phosphorus is very unlikely.

Potassium (K) or the compound potash (K_2O) increases foliage chlorophyll and helps plants make better use of light and air. It encourages strong root growth and is associated with disease resistance and water intake.

A lack of potassium makes plants grow slowly and is not easy to detect. Signs are that leaves have mottled yellow blades and fringes. Older leaves may appear scorched on the edges, also new growth may die back. Do not confuse these symptoms with salt or fertilizer burn, which causes burned leaf tips that may curl under. (See color section). The potassium is usually present in the soil, but locked in by high salinity. First, leach the toxic salt out of the soil, then apply foliar N-P-K fertilizer.

Excess potassium is very unlikely. About one percent of the potassium in the soil is available to plants. Insoluble potassium is found in organic matter and minerals. It moves within the soil slowly.

Secondary nutrient deficiencies are easily avoided by mixing one cup of fine dolomite lime per cubic foot of soil before planting. Dolomite supplies soil with magnesium and calcium. Magnesium (Mg) is found in every chlorophyll molecule and is essential to the absorption of light energy. Magnesium aids in the utilization of nutrients. It also neutralizes soil acids and toxic compounds produced by the plant. It is the only secondary nutrient that is commonly found deficient. Adding dolomite lime before planting will stabilize pH and add magnesium and calcium to the soil. Add Epsom salts (soluble magnesium) with each watering if no dolomite was added when planting.

Calcium (Ca) is essential to cell manufacture and plant growth. Plants must have calcium at the growing tip of each root. The easiest way to supply calcium is to add steamed bone meal or colloidal phosphate to the soil when planting.

If too much calcium is applied early in life, it might stunt growth as well. Signs of deficiency dare a yellowing and dying back of leaf edges. Mixing fine dolomite lime with the soil before planting is the best prevention of this ailment. If you must, use a trace element formula containing calcium to treat the deficiency.

Trace elements are essential for plant growth and must be present in minute amounts, but little is known about the exact amounts that are needed. They also function as catalysts to plant processes and nutrient utilization. Important trace elements include iron (Fe), sulfur (S), manganese (Mn), boron (B), molybdenum (Mo), zinc (Zn), and copper (Cu). Trace elements are usually in most soils. However, extreme acidity or alkalinity may make them unavailable to plants. Liberal applications of compost or organic matter of all kinds will often remedy this problem.

Symptoms of secondary and trace element deficiencies for specific plants are found under their individual listings.

Sulfur (S) is almost never a problem for soils able to grow marijuana. Many fertilizers contain some form of sulfur. Deficiency shows when leaves turn pale green and general purpose N-P-K fertilizer fails to cure the problem. Very seldom is it a problem, but if it is, remedy with trace element fertilizer.

Iron (Fe) - deficiency is somewhat common. An iron deficient (chlorotic) leaf is yellowing between the veins while the veins remain green. Leaves may start to fall if it is severe. Chlorosis is generally caused by a high pH rather than a lack of iron. To remedy, correct pH. If necessary, foliar feed with fertilizer containing soluble chelated iron.

Other micro-nutrients, manganese, boron, molybdenum, zinc and copper, are rarely deficient in any soil. By using commercial potting soil, fortified soilless mix, or N-P-K fertilizer with trace elements, you are guaranteed that all necessary trace elements are available. Fertilizers that contain only trace elements are available, but may be very tricky to use. Trace elements are necessary in minute amounts and reach toxic levels easily.

Nutrient Disorders

There are many things that could go wrong that are confused with a lack of fertilizer. The pH of both the growing medium and water is of prime importance. If the pH is not between 6.5 and 7, some nutrients will be locked in the soil, even if the nutrients are present. The plant is not able to absorb nutrients chemically because the pH will not let it. A pH below 6.5 may cause a deficiency in calcium. If this happens, root tips could burn and leaves could get fungus (leaf spot). A pH over 7 could slow down the plant's iron intake; chlorotic leaves with yellowing veins could result.

Incorrect pH contributes to most serious nutrient disorders. I am always amazed so many people worry about fertilizer application and do not pay attention to the pH!

Nutrient deficiencies seldom occur in fresh potting soil or a good organic mix containing dolomite lime.

Chlorosis = iron deficiency. When iron is lacking, nitrogen cannot be absorbed properly. This is why leaves turn lime green toward the veins. Remedy chlorosis by adding chelated (available) iron to fertilizer mixes.

Over-fertilizing causes a build up of nutrients (salts) to reach toxic levels and changes soil chemistry. When plants are over-fertilized, growth is rapid and lush green until the toxic levels are reached. When the toxic salt (fertilizer) level is reached, leaf tips burn, (turn yellow, then black), and if the problem is severe, the leaves will curl under like a claw.

Chance of over-fertilization is greater when growing in small containers.

To treat severely over-fertilized plants, leach soil with 2 gallons of water per gallon of soil, so as to wash all the excess nutrients out. The plant should start new growth and look better in one or two weeks. If the problem is severe, and leaves are curled, the soil may need to be leached several times. After the plant resumes normal growth, start foliar feeding or apply diluted fertilizer solution.

Organic Fertilizers

Organic nutrients, manure, worm castings, blood and bone meal, etc., work very well to increase the soil nutrient content, but nutrients are released and available at different rates. The nutrient availability may be difficult to calculate, but it is hard to over-apply organic fertilizers. Organic nutrients work best when used in combination with one another to provide more consistent availability of nutrients.

Organic gardens in containers use potting soil high in worm castings, peat, sand, manure, leaf mold, compost and fine dolomite lime. In a container, there is little space to build the soil by mixing composts and organic nutrients. It is easiest and less problematic to throw out old depleted soil and start new plants with fresh organic soil.

Many of the organic nutrients are available in the form of animal feed and can be purchased at feed stores. Animals consume many of the same foods as plants. For example, alfalfa meal, rich in available nitrogen, is found in the form of alfalfa hay or pellets for rabbit, horse or cattle feed. All feed stores have alfalfa pellets. Go to the livestock feed store and check out their products. You will certainly find many new fertilizers.

Alfalfa meal is rich in nitrogen, containing about 2.5 percent and 5 percent phosphorus and about 2 percent potash. This nutrient can be cultivated into the soil's surface for excellent results. Nitrogen is released relatively quickly, within 4 weeks.

Blood (dried or meal) is collected at slaughterhouses, dried and ground into a powder or meal. It is an excellent source of fast-acting soluble nitrogen (12 to 15 percent by weight), about 1.2 percent phosphorus and under one percent potash. Apply just before planting or as a side dressing to stimulate green leafy growth. It can burn plants if set on foliage or applied too heavily. Blood meal attracts meat-eating animals, so always cultivate it into the soil if using as a side dressing.

Bone meal is an old-time fertilizer that is rich in phosphorus and nitrogen. The age and type of bone determine the nutrient content of this pulverized slaughterhouse product. Older bones have a higher phosphorus content than young bones. Use bone meal in conjunction with other organic fertilizers for best results. Its lime content helps reduce soil acidity, and acts fastest in well-aerated soil.

Raw, unsteamed bone meal contains 2 to 4 percent nitrogen and 15 to 25 percent phosphorus. Fatty acids in raw bone meal require longer to decompose.

Steamed or cooked bone meal is made from fresh animal bones that have been boiled or steamed under pressure to render out fats. The pressure treatment causes a little nitrogen loss and an increase in phosphorus. Steamed bones are easier to grind into a fine powder and the process helps nutrients become available sooner. It contains up to 30 percent phosphorus and about 1.5 percent nitrogen. Finer bone meal is faster acting. Apply as a seasonal source of phosphorus to the soil when planting or to flowering plants as a late summer top dressing that is lightly cultivated into the soil and covered with mulch.

Cottonseed meal is made from shelled cotton seed that has had the oil extracted. According to the manufacturer, virtually all chemical residues from commercial cotton production are dissolved in the oil. This acidic fertilizer contains about 7 percent nitrogen, 2.5 percent phosphorus and 1.5 percent potash. It should be supplemented with pulverized rock phosphate or bone meal to form a balanced fertilizer blend.

Chicken manure is a favorite of many gardeners because it is so high in nitrogen. If you can find a good source of chicken manure, get as much as you can. Pile it up next to the compost pile, let it rot for a couple of months then cover it with a tarp to slow decomposition. Use it as a compost activator, or as a top or side dressing as often as possible. If the manure comes from a commercial chicken ranch that uses growth hormones, let it compost at least a year so the hormones are washed out or "fixed". Many times chicken manure is full of feathers that contain as much as 17 percent nitrogen, which is an added bonus. The average nutrient content of wet chicken manure is: N - 1.5%, P - 1.5%, K - 0.5% and dry: N - 4%, P - 4%, K - 1.5% and both have a full range of trace elements.

Compost tea is used by numerous organic gardeners as the only source of fertilizer.

Comfrey is packed with nutrients and many gardeners grow it

just to add to their compost tea.

Cow manure is sold as "steer" manure but it is collected from dairy herds. Gardeners have had access to and used cow manure for centuries and this has led to the belief that it is a good fertilizer as well as a soil amendment. Steer manure is most valuable as a mulch and a soil amendment, it holds water well and maintains fertility for a long time. The nutrient value is low and should not be relied upon for the main source of nitrogen. The average nutrient content of cow manure is N - 0.6%, P - 0.3%, K - 0.3% and a full range of trace elements. Apply at the rate of 25 - 30 pounds per square yard of soil.

Coffee grounds are acidic and encourage acetic-acid-bacteria in the soil. Drip coffee grounds are the richest, containing about 2 percent nitrogen, and traces of other nutrients. Add to the compost pile or scatter and cultivate in as a top dressing to acidify soil.

Diatomaceous earth, the fossilized skeletal remains of fresh and salt water algae, contains a full range of 14 chelated trace elements and is a good insecticide. The many sharp facets on DE cut insects and their body fluids leak out. Apply to the soil when cultivating or as a top dressing.

Dolomite lime adjusts and balances the pH and makes phosphates more available, generally applied to "sweeten" or de-acidify soil. It consists of calcium and magnesium, sometimes listed as primary nutrients but here referred to as the secondary nutrients.

Feathers and feather meal contain from 12 to 15 percent nitrogen that is released slowly. Feathers included in barnyard chicken manure or obtained from slaughterhouses are an excellent addition to the compost pile or as a fertilizer. Feathers are steamed under pressure, dried, then ground into a powdery feather meal. Feather meal contains about 12.5 percent slow-release nitrogen. Apply in the fall for nitrogen-rich soil the following spring.

Fish meal is made from dried fish that is ground into a meal. It is rich in nitrogen (about 8 percent) and contains around 7 percent phosphoric acid and many trace elements. It has an unpleasant odor and should not be used indoors. Fish meal is a great compost activator. Apply to the soil as a relatively fast-acting side or top dressing. Make sure to cultivate it into the soil or cover with mulch after applying. Always store in an air tight container so it will not attract cats, dogs and flies. Fish meal and fish emulsion can contain up to 10 percent nitrogen. The liquid generally contains less nitrogen than the meal. Even when deodorized, the liquid form has an unpleasant odor. Inorganic potash is added to fish meal by some manufacturers and is "semi-organic."

Make your own fish emulsion by grinding fish up before putting them in the garden. Also, you can bury fish carcasses in the planting hole. I recommend 2 - 4 carcasses from12 - 16" in length per large hole.

Fish emulsion, an inexpensive soluble liquid, is high in organic nitrogen, trace elements and some phosphorus and potassium. This natural fertilizer is difficult to over-apply and is immediately available to plants. Fish emulsion may be diluted with water and used as a foliar spray, but may clog small nozzles if mixed too rich. Even deodorized fish emulsion smells, or use only on outdoor plants.

Goat manure is much like horse manure, but more potent. Compost this manure and treat it as you would horse manure. See below.

Granite dust or granite stone meal contains up to 5 percent potash, and several trace elements. Releasing nutrients slowly over several years, granite dust is an inexpensive source of potash and does not affect soil pH. Apply as a top dressing, or at the rate of ten to fifteen pounds per 100 square feet. Combine granite dust with phosphate rock and manure for a complete fertilizer mix to start crops in the spring.

Greensand (glaucomite) is an iron potassium silicate that gives the minerals in which it occurs a green tint. It is mined from an ancient sea bed in New Jersey. The sea bed deposit of shells and organic material rich in iron, phosphorus, potash (5 to 7 percent) and numerous micronutrients. Greensand does not burn plants, slowly releasing its treasures in about four years. Apply greensand as a top dressing or blend with soil at the rate of 15 to 25 pounds per 100 square feet any time of year as a long-term source of potassium and trace elements.

Guano (bat) consists of the droppings and remains of bats. It is rich in soluble nitrogen, phosphorus and trace elements. The limited supply of this fertilizer, known as the soluble organic super bloom, makes it expensive. Mined in sheltered caves, guano dries with minimal decomposition. Bat guano can be thousands of years old. Newer deposits contain high levels of nitrogen and are capable of burning if applied too heavily. The more popular older deposits are high in phosphorus and make an excellent flowering fertilizer. Bat guano is usually powdery and used as a top dressing or diluted in a tea and used as a foliar spray. Do not breathe the dust when handling; it can cause nausea and irritation. Bats are too often associated with rabies and horror movies. Only ten cases of rabies have been reported in the U.S. from bat bites. Some bats eat thousands of insects nightly, others live on rotting fruit. These seemingly prehistoric creatures are invaluable to the ecosystem and must be protected. Bat guano may be difficult to find at retail stores, however, several suppliers listed in garden magazines stock bat guano.

Guano (sea bird) is high in nitrogen and other nutrients. The Humboldt Current along the coast of Peru and northern Chile keeps the rain from falling and decomposition of the guano is minimal. South American guano is among the world's best. The guano is scraped off the rocks of arid sea islands. The average dose is one tablespoon per gallon of water. Guano is also collected from many coastlines around the world.

Gypsum, hydrated calcium sulfate, is used to lower soil pH and improve drainage and aeration. It is also used to hold or slow the rapid decomposition of nitrogen.

Hoof and horn meal is a coarse granular substance that is an excellent source of slow release nitrogen. The drawback of this meal is that it draws flies and encourages maggots. Soil bacteria must break it down before it is available to roots. Apply two to three weeks before planting. It remains in soil for six months or longer. Hoof and horn meal contains from 6 to 15 percent nitrogen and about 2 percent phosphoric acid. Finely ground horn meal, on the other hand, makes the nitrogen available quicker, and has few problems with fly maggots.

Horse manure is readily available from horse stables and race tracks. Use horse manure that has hemp, straw or peat for bedding. Wood shavings (except cedar) could be a source of plant disease. Compost horse manure for two months or more before adding to the garden. The composting process kills weed seeds and makes nutrients available in soluble form. Straw bedding may also use up much of the available nitrogen to speed decomposition. But the straw makes a lot of air space within the manure so it can be piled quite high without adding other materials to provide aeration. Nutrient content of horse manure N - 0.6%, P - 0.6%, K - 0.4% and a full range of trace elements.

Kelp is the "Cadillac™ of trace minerals." Kelp should be deep green, fresh and smell like the ocean. Seaweed contains 60 to 70 trace minerals that are already chelated (existing in a form that's water-soluble and mobile in the soil).

Oyster shells are ground and normally used as a calcium source for poultry. They contain up to 55 percent calcium, and traces of many other nutrients that release slowly. Add finely ground oyster shells to compost or in small amounts with other fertilizers when cultivating to ensure adequate calcium content.

Paper ash contains about 5 percent phosphorus and over 2 percent potash. It is an excellent water soluble fertilizer, but do not apply in large doses because the pH is quite high.

Pigeon manure has a very high concentration of nitrogen but is more difficult to find. It can be used just like chicken manure.

Rabbit manure is an excellent fertilizer but is difficult to find in large quantities. Use rabbit manure as you would chicken or pigeon manure.

Rock phosphate (hard) is a calcium or lime based phosphate rock that is finely ground to the consistency of talcum powder. This rock powder contains over 30 percent phosphates and a collection of trace elements. It does not leach out of the soil, remaining unchanged until taken up by roots. Apply at the rate of ten pounds per 100 square feet of soil every four or five years a couple of months after applying annual manure.

Colloidal phosphate, also called powdered or soft phosphate, which is a natural clay phosphate deposit that contains just over 20 percent phosphorus (P_2O_5), calcium and many trace elements. Colloidal phosphate is an excellent value in organic fertilizers. It yields 2 percent phosphate by weight the first season and a total of 18 percent over the next several years. Soft phosphate will not burn and is available to plants as needed. It is also a good soil builder that encourages earthworms and beneficial soil microbes. Cultivate soft phosphate into the soil annually at the rate of five pounds per 100 square feet of soil in conjunction with lime and nitrogen-rich manures and seaweed meal. Or till in 15 to 20 pounds of soft phosphate per 100 square feet along with lime every four years.

Rock potash is an important source of potassium. It releases very slowly and stays in the soil for several years. Potash rock supplies up to 8 percent potassium and may contain many trace elements.

Seaweed meal or kelp meal is harvested from the ocean or picked up along beaches, cleansed of salty water, dried and ground into a powdery meal. It is packed full of potassium (potash) numerous trace elements, vitamins, amino acids and plant hormones. The nutrient content varies according to the type of kelp and its growing conditions. Seaweed meal is easily assimilated by plants and contributes to soil life, structure and nitrogen fixation. It may also help plants resist many diseases and withstand light frosts. Apply the dry powder at the rate of one or two pounds per 100 square feet of garden soil in the spring for best results. Allow several weeks for soil bacteria to make nutrients available. Kelp meal also speeds compost decomposition and eases transplant shock.

Seaweed (liquid) contains nitrogen, phosphorus, potash, all necessary trace elements that are chelated (existing in a form that's water-soluble and mobile in the soil) and plant hormones. Apply dilute solution to the soil or use as a foliar spray for a quick cure of nutrient deficiencies. Liquid seaweed is also great for soaking seeds and dipping cuttings or bare roots before planting.

Sheep manure, normally found indoors in the sheep pens, is rich in nutrients and makes a wonderful nutrient tea. The average nutrient content is: N - 0.8%, P - 0.5%, K - 0.4% and a full range of trace elements. Sheep manures are hot because they contain little water and lots of air. They heat up readily in a compost pile. Cow and pig manures are cold because they hold a lot of water and can be compacted easily, squeezing out the air.

Shrimp & crab wastes contain relatively high levels of phosphorus.

Swine manure has a high nutrient content but is slower acting and wetter than cow and horse manure. The average nutrient content of pig manure is: N - 0.6%, P - 0.6%, K - 0.4% and a full range of trace elements.

Wood ashes (hardwood) supply up to 10 percent potash and softwood ashes contain about 5 percent. Potash leaches rapidly, so collect ash soon after burning and store in a dry place. Apply in a mix with other fertilizers at the rate of five or ten pounds per 100 square feet. The potash washes out of heavy layers of wood ash quickly and cause compacted, sticky soil. Wood ash makes an excellent addition to compost piles.

Worm castings are digested humus and other organic matter that contain varying amounts of N-P-K. They are an excellent source of non-burning soluble nitrogen that is available immediately. Worm castings are also an excellent soil additive that promote fertility and soil structure. Mix with potting soil to form a rich, fertile blend. Worm castings, when pure, look like coarse graphite powder. They are high in available nitrogen as well as many other nutrients. Worm castings are used as an organic fertilizer and soil amendment. Earthworms eat and digest decomposing organic matter. The castings are this excreted organic matter. Worm castings are heavy and very dense. When mixing with soil, use no more than 30 percent worm castings. They are so heavy, root growth can be impaired. Most nurseries do not stock worm castings. Check the newspaper and ask at the nursery for possible sources.

Note: The nutrients in organic fertilizers may vary greatly depending upon source, age, erosion, climate, etc. For exact nutrient content, consult the vendor's specifications.

Four Basic Organic Fertilizer Mixes

2 - 4 - 3:
1 part bone meal, 3 parts chopped hay, 2 parts greensand.

3 - 3 - 4:
3 parts fine granite dust, 1 part blood meal, 1 part bone meal,
5 parts seaweed meal.

4 - 5 - 4:
2 parts blood meal, 1 part soft phosphate, 4 parts hardwood ashes.

4 - 6 - 4:
2 parts cottonseed meal, 1 part soft phosphate, 1 part fine granite
dust.

*Manure or other soluble organic fertilizers are diluted in water to make
manure tea. This tea is an excellent fertilizer that can be used often. Dry
fertilizer is much easier to carry than liquid. Growers "band" dry fertilizers
around plants and cultivate into the soil to activate.*

Organic Tea

Organic fertilizer tea concoctions contain soluble organic nutrients diluted in water. Fish emulsion and liquid seaweed are readily available commercial organic tea concentrates. Soluble fertilizers, including worm castings, manures and guanos, make excellent U-mix organic teas. Any soluble organic nutrient can be soaked in a barrel of water and made into a tea. The nutrient(s) are mixed with water, left to sit for a few days, and then applied. Or the fertilizers can be placed in a (tea) bag in a barrel. A dilute tea may be applied as often as each watering. Make sure you stir the tea before applying. The tea bag works best with soluble organic fertilizers including: bat guano, fish emulsion, sea guano, seaweed and worm castings.

Hydroponic Gardening

Hydroponic gardening, growing plants without soil in a soilless mix, allows control of the nutrient and oxygen intake via roots.

In hydroponics, the inert soilless medium contains no nutrients of its own. All the nutrients are supplied by the nutrient solution. This solution passes over the roots or floods around them at regular intervals, later draining off. The extra oxygen around roots speeds uptake of nutrients. They are able to take in food as fast as they are able to utilize it. In soil, as in hydroponics, the roots absorb nutrients and water; even the best soil rarely has as much oxygen in it as a soilless hydroponic medium.

Hydroponic gardening is very exacting, and not forgiving like soil gardening. The soil works as a buffer for nutrients and holds them longer than the inert medium of hydroponics.

Growing marijuana hydroponically outdoors requires a secure growing area and an ample supply of water. Most outdoor growers do not have access to adequate water or a totally secure growing area. For more information on hydroponics please consult *Indoor Marijuana Horticulture* by Jorge Cervantes (available in Dutch, English and German), *Marijuana Indoors: Five Easy Gardens*, by Jorge Cervantes or *Hydroponic Food Production* (available in Spanish/English) by Howard Resh.

Pests and Diseases - Insects & Fungus

Insects live everywhere outdoors. Their populations explode when the weather conditions are right, usually warm and humid. Fungus is present in the air at all times and will settle and grow if climatic conditions are right. Both fungus and insects can be prevented, but once an infestation has started, severe methods of control may be necessary to eradicate them.

Prevention

Cleanliness is the first step to insect and fungus prevention. Keep decaying debris off soil surface. Do not use mulch if insects and fungus are a problem.

Do you and your tools could transport many microscopic bugs and fungi that may be fatal to the garden. Insects and fungus love to ride from plant to plant on dirty tools. Disinfect tools by dipping them in rubbing alcohol, or wash with soap and water after using them on a diseased plant. Wash your hands before handling plants and after handling diseased plants. Do not visit insect infested gardens, then go right to work in your clean indoor garden.

Once you have grown a container crop in a potting soil or soilless mix, throw out the soil. Some growers place charcoal in the bottom of containers to absorb excess salts and maintain sweet soil. Used soil in containers may harbor harmful insects and fungi. Starting a new crop in new potting soil will cost more up front, but will eliminate many potential problems.

If growing in large planting holes outdoors, throwing out the soil is unnecessary and impractical. This soil only needs to be amended again after harvest, covered with mulch and left to lay fallow all winter. When planted in the spring, the soil will be better than new!

Companion planting helps discourage insects. Most insects hate garlic. When sowing seeds or transplanting, just plant a few cloves of garlic about ½" deep with them. Garlic will grow straight up, creating very little shade, and has a compact root system attached to the bulb below the soil. When transplanting, move garlic along with the marijuana. Companion plants also use water. If your garden is in a drought area, companion plants may use too much water to be viable.

Plant insect and fungus resistant varieties of marijuana.

Keep plants healthy and growing fast at all times. Disease attacks sickly plants first. Strong plants tend to grow faster than bugs can eat or fungus can spread. Strong, healthy, fast growing plants have few insect and fungus problems. Make life miserable for bugs and fungus. Insects hate wind and a spray of water. Fungus has little time to settle in a breeze and does not grow well on wind-dried soil, stems and leaves.

Insects and Spider Mites

Gardeners have many options open for insect and fungi control. Prevention and cleanliness are at the top of the list, followed by climate control. Next comes physically removing insects by smashing them or picking them off foliage. If spraying, use natural substances. Harsh chemicals are a last resort. Even natural sprays seem to slow growth. Sprays cover foliage with filmy residue. Wash residue off a few days after spraying for best results. The stronger the spray, the harder it is on the plant. Spray plants as little as possible and do not spray at all for two weeks before harvest. Read the labels of all insecticides and fungicides thoroughly before you use them.

Use only use contact sprays approved for edible plants. Do not use sprays on young seedlings or clones. It could burn or kill tender little plants.

Sprays to Kill Insects and Mites

Bacillus thuringiensis (*BT*) is the best known of several bacteria that attack the larval forms of insects. Other related microbial insecticides are *B. lentimorbus* and *B. sphaericus*. *Bt/H-14* sold under the trade names Vectobac and Gnatrol in the US controls destructive soil nematodes. Destructive nematodes are difficult to see. They cause slow plant growth and slowly rotting roots.

Caterpillars and worms eat the *BT* bacteria that is applied to the surface of the foliage and within a short time their digestive systems are poisoned.

More than a half dozen different strains of *BT* are common today. *B. thuringiensis* var. *kurstaki* (*BTK*) is toxic to many moth and caterpillar larvae, including many of the species that feed on *cannabis*. *B. thuringiensis* var. *israelensis* (*BTI*) is effective against the larvae of mosquitoes, black flies and fungus gnats.

Since *BT* usually does not produce spores within insect bodies, several applications may be necessary to control an insect pest infestation.

Diatomaceous Earth

DE is fatal to most soft-bodied insects including aphids, slugs, and spider mites. DE also contains 14 trace minerals in a chelated (available) form. DE is not registered as a pesticide or fungicide; recommendations are based on the research and observations of expert growers. When dusted on plants and soil, DE abrades the waxy coating on pest shells or skin, allowing body fluids to leak out. If the pest ingests the razor-sharp diatomaceous earth, it acts similarly on the creature's gut. Earthworms, animals, humans and birds can digest diatomaceous earth with no ill effects. Use a protective mask and goggles when handling this fine powder to guard against respiratory and eye irritations.

Mix 1 part DE with 3 to 5 parts water and a few drops of biodegradable dish soap to use as a spray. Apply this spray to infestations of pest insects.

Caution! Do not use swimming pool diatomaceous earth.

Chemically treated and heated, it contains crystalline silica that is very hazardous if inhaled. The body is unable to dissolve the crystalline form of silica, which causes chronic irritation.

Homemade Sprays

Many homemade spray preparations repel and kill *cannabis* pests. A strong hot taste or smelly odor are the main principles behind most home-brewed potions.

The sprays are normally made by mixing repellent plants with a little water in a blender. The resulting slurry concentrate should be strained through a nylon stocking or fine cheesecloth before being diluted with water for application, either will keep it from clogging a sprayer.

Cooking or heating preparations generally destroys active ingredients. To draw out ingredients, mince plant and soak in mineral oil for a couple of days. Add this oil to the water including a little detergent or soap to emulsify (suspend) the oil droplets in water. Biodegradable detergents and soaps are good wetting and sticking agents for these preparations. Soap dissolves best if a teaspoon of alcohol is also added to each quart of water.

Chrysanthemum, marigold, and nasturtium blossoms; pennyroyal, garlic, chive, onion, hot pepper, insect juice (target insects mixed in a blender), horseradish, mints, oregano, tomato, and tobacco residues all repel or kill insects including aphids, caterpillars, mites, and whiteflies. Mixes can vary in proportions, but always filter the blended slurry before mixing with water for the final spray. One good recipe is 1 teaspoon of hot pepper or Tabasco sauce and 4 cloves of garlic blended with a quart of water. Grind this mix up in the blender and strain through a nylon stocking or cheese cloth before using in the sprayer.

A mix of one-eighth cup of hydrated lime mixed with a quart of water makes an effective insect spray, especially on tiny pests such as spider mites. Mix a nondetergent soap with the lime; the soap acts as both a sticking agent and insecticide. Lime can be caustic in large doses. Always try the spray on a test plant and wait a few days to check for adverse effects to the plant before applying to similar plants.

Sprays that include chamomile plant parts are used to prevent damping-off and mildew. Liquid laundry bleach (sodium hypochlorite) is a good fungicide. Usually sold as a five percent solution, it is an eye and skin irritant; wear gloves and goggles when using it. Mix 1 part bleach to 9 parts water and use this solution as a general disinfectant for greenhouse equipment, tools, and plant wounds. The bleach solution breaks down rapidly and therefore has

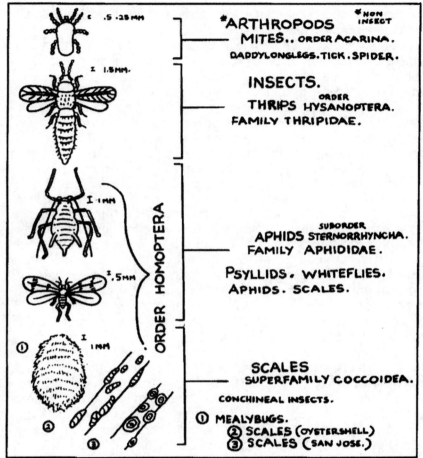

Insects cause less trouble to outdoor plants than indoor plants. Always check for insect and fungus damage. If any signs occur, see text, control as soon as possible.

little if any residual effect. Growers who don't like bleach use a 35 percent solution of H_2O_2 solution.

Insecticidal Soaps

Insecticidal soaps are mild contact insecticides made from fatty acids of animals and plants. These soaps are safe for bees, animals, and humans. The soap controls soft-bodied insects such as aphids, mealybugs, spider mites, thrips, and whiteflies by penetrating and clogging body membranes.

Safer's Insecticidal Soap is a well-known commercial product. It is a potassium-salt based liquid concentrate that is toxic to insects but not to animals or humans. It is most effective when applied at the first appearance of insects pests.

Soft soaps made with biodegradable soap and kill insects in a similar manner as insecticidal soap, but they are not as potent. Do not use detergent soaps as they may be caustic. Mix a few capfuls of one of these soaps to a quart of water to make a spray.

These soaps can also be used as a wetting agent when watering down peat moss, dry potting soil, or seedlings. Both soap and detergent reduce the surface tension of the water to give better penetration. Soaps can also be used as a spreader-sticker to mix with sprays. Soft soaps last only for about one day before dissipating.

Nicotine (sulfate) is a non-persistent pesticide derived from tobacco. It is toxic to most insects and humans if a concentrate is swallowed. This very poisonous compound affects the neuromuscular system, causing insects to go into convulsions and die. Often nicotine is mixed with sulfur to form nicotine sulfate.

Horticultural oil sprays, widely used in greenhouses, are not the same kinds of oils used in the car nor sold at the hardware store. Horticultural oil is refined by removing most of the portion that is toxic to plants. Petroleum oils smother bugs and eggs, as well as generally impair their life cycle. Use only lightweight horticultural oil with a viscosity of 60 - 70. Lightweight oil is less toxic to plants. I prefer to use oil sprays only during vegetative growth so the residue has time to dissipate before harvest. Mix two drops of oil spray (no more than a 1 percent solution) per quart of water. More than a few drops could burn tender growing shoots and clog leaf pores. Repeat applications as needed, usually 3 applications, one every 5 to 10 days will do it. The first application will get most of the adults and many eggs. Eggs hatch in about 10 days. The second spraying will kill the newly hatched eggs and the remaining adults. The third application will finish off any survivors.

Neem oil, while relatively new in the US, has been used for many years as a botanical insecticide in Africa and southeast Asia where the neem tree (Azadirachta indica) is native. Neem oil extract is an effective control for dozens of insect pests, including leafminers, mealybugs, whiteflies, caterpillars, crickets, and grasshoppers.

Neem oil acts as both a contact pesticide and a systemic. When bitter, strong-smelling neem oil is added to the soil, the essential ingredients become systemic, entering the plants stems and foliage. Pests then either pass up the bitter, strong smelling plant parts, or eat them and die before maturing.

Neem oil has very low toxicity to mammals. The active ingredients break down rapidly in sunlight and within a few weeks in the soil.

Pyrethrum is an extremely powerful broad spectrum pesticide that is very toxic to most insects, including those that are beneficial. Applied as a spray, pyrethrum is a very effective control of flying insects. Pyrethrum is sometimes combined with rotenone or ryania to ensure effectiveness. Use this non-selective insecticide to spot spray only heavily infested plants.

Pyrethrum is not toxic to animals or humans. Purchase in aerosol, dust or liquid. Aerosol spray is very convenient, but can burn foliage if applied closer than one foot. Aerosols also contain piperonyl butoxide which is toxic to people. All forms of pyrethrum dissipate within a few hours in the presence of air and sunlight. At least one manufacturer offers encapsulated pyrethrum in aerosol form. As the spray fogs out of the nozzle, a bubble forms around each droplet of pyrethrum. The bubble coating keeps the pyrethrum intact for several days. If an insect should encounter the bubble, pop, the pyrethrum is released.

It is almost impossible to incorrectly apply the aerosol/fogger, except for standing too close. The pyrethrum shoots out in a fog and goes everywhere, even to the bottoms of the leaves, anywhere bugs can hide! Make sure to follow the manufacturers directions.

Synthetic pyrethroids are toxic to honeybees.

Rotenone, Ryania and Sabadilla are often mixed together and sold under various brand names. All are plant extracts applied as a spray (wettable powder), or dust. These non-selective contact insecticide are stomach or nerve poisons are very effective against beetles, caterpillars, flies, grasshoppers, mosquitoes, thrips, weevils and beneficial insects.

They do not harm plants, and wont linger in the soil. Residues break down in three to seven days in the presence of light and air. Use this spray only as a last resort, and be careful not to let it wash into garden pools or streams, as it is extremely toxic to fish. It is also toxic to birds and pigs.

Sulfur is a common fungicide that has been used for centuries. Sulfur dust, wettable sulfur, and sulfur in large particles are the three main forms. Commercial products that add copper and oils to the sulfur are more potent than sulfur alone against plant diseases. For that reason, don't use the commercial combination if you plan to apply oil sprays within a month. Avoid scorching foliage by never applying sulfur when temperatures are above 85 to 90 degrees F. Sulfur is a useful insecticide as well as a fungicide. It is toxic to insects and even more toxic to mites.

Traps

Sticky traps such as flypaper or Tanglefoot™ are very effective.

Sticky resins or other sticky materials can be smeared on attractive yellow or red objects to simulate ripe fruit. When the pests land on the fruit they are stuck forever! Tanglefoot™ can also be used as a barrier on pots and plant stems and trunks. Insects are unable to cross the barrier and move from one plant or pot to the next.

Predators

Beneficial Insects are predatory insects which are usually equipped with crushing or piercing jaws and are larger, stronger, and more agile than their prey. Predatory larvae search out and devour insects and many are more ferocious predators than their parents.

Parasites eat pest insects from the inside: Adults lay eggs in or on the host, the eggs hatch, the larva emerge and once inside the host, begin to feed. Some host insects die within 48 hours while others take several weeks. Most hosts get sick and quit eating within 24 hours of the parasite entering the body. Some parasites release a bacteria that kills the host.

Beneficial insects are attracted by the blooms (which supply pollen and nectar) of a wide variety of plants, such as alfalfa, candytuft, carrot, coriander, fennel, ox-eye daisy, goldenrod, Queen Annes lace, white and sweet clover, and yarrow.

Indiscriminate use of broad spectrum insecticides (even botanical ones such as pyrethrum and rotenone) kill all insects including predators that are beneficial. Therefore, limit spraying of any pesticides, herbicides, insecticides, or fungicides to spot applications when more conservative measures do not work.

Predatory insects include centipedes, beetles, firefly larvae or glowworms, lacewings, ladybugs, mealybug destroyers, beneficial nematodes, praying mantis, spiders, and parasitic wasps.

Large Pest Predators

Encourage the following large predators to patrol your garden. They will consume large numbers of plant pests.

The number of insects that bats catch each night is close to their body weight. Among their targets are numerous night-flying moths. Many of these moths are develop from destructive caterpillars. Ponds will attract insects which will in turn attract bats.

Birds consume caterpillars, aphids, and many other insects. Many wild birds are omnivores, eating both plants (usually fruit and seeds) and animals (usually insects) in season. Entice these predators by having birdhouses, birdseed, suet, bird baths, and plants for cover in the garden. Some insect-eating birds include: bluebirds, chickadees, titmice, mockingbirds, orioles, purple martins, robins, thrushes, warblers, and wrens.

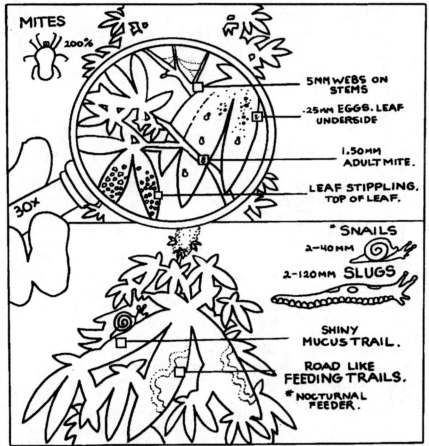

MITES
100%
30x

5MM WEBS ON STEMS
.25MM EGGS. LEAF UNDERSIDE
1.50MM ADULT MITE.
LEAF STIPPLING. TOP OF LEAF.

* SNAILS
2-40MM
2-120MM SLUGS
SHINY MUCUS TRAIL.
ROAD LIKE FEEDING TRAILS.
* NOCTURNAL FEEDER.

Mites leave tell-tale whitish spots on leaves. Actual mites are found on leaf underside. Snails and slugs dissolve and consume foliage. Look for tell-tale slimy mucus trails.

Barn **owls** can clean out a population of gophers in just a few nights. Owls also eat many nocturnal mice and voles.

Moles and shrews eat insects, larvae and slugs.

Frogs and toads are relentless insect and slug predators. Most frogs live and breed in or near water. Toads require a relatively natural setting with cool hiding places.

Large **snakes** eat gophers, moles, squirrels and mice. Smaller snakes eat slugs and insects. Lizards and salamanders also eat insects and other pests. Attract snakes, lizards, and salamanders with cool, covered areas for habitat.

What's Eating My Plants?

To find what's eating plants, examine plant foliage and surrounding area carefully. If necessary, take a close look at them with a microscope. Normally a 30X microscope will make the insects large enough for the untrained eye to see.

Insects & Other Small Pests

Aphids, or plant lice, include many species. These insects are about the size of a pin head and can be green, yellow and red. Some have wings, but most do not. Aphids puncture foliage and suck out plant fluids.

They are most common on sickly over-fertilized with nitrogen plants. Look on leaf undersides and soft plant parts. Aphids excrete a sticky honeydew that transmits viral diseases and molds.

Interplanting with anise, chives, coriander, garlic, nasturtiums and petunias repels aphids.

Control aphids by smashing between fingers or blast off foliage with a jet of water. Ladybugs, lacewings and hoverfly larvae are aphid preditors.

Homemade lime-juice sprays, hot pepper sprays or tobacco sprays kill aphids. So do commercial insecticidal soaps and pyrethrum sprays.

Borers are the larvae of insects that tunnel or bore through stems or trunks. They cause the foliage on the branch or stem to wilt. Look for a small entry hole and moist sawdust castings on stems.

A dusting of black pepper or camphor around the base of plants repels egg-laying moths. Control most borers by pruning branches below the damaged area and destroying the branches.

Caterpillars and Loppers are worms that measure up to an inch and a half long. Green, sometimes striped loppers, double up as they crawl around, chewing holes in leaves.

Control cabbage loopers by hand-picking, or spray with insecticidal soap, lime spray, or BT. As a last resort, use rotenone or a pyrethrum insecticide.

Cutworms are plump, brown to light green ½ to 1 ½-inch-long worms (caterpillars or larvae) that coil up when disturbed. Cutworms live just below the soil's surface feeding at the bases of plants, cutting them off at soil level. Adults turn into night-flying moths.

If you mysteriously find dead plants immediately search just under the surface of the soil around the base of the dead plant. Cutworms usually linger at the scene of the crime. Dig around the stem 1/2 inch deep to search out and destroy them. If you wait several days, the cutworm could be several feet away and very difficult to find.

Prevent cutworm damage by sprinkling corn meal, chicken manure, crushed eggshells, or moist wood ashes around the bases of plants. Control with a dusting of diatomaceous earth or BT.

Grasshoppers not only eat and gnaw through leaves and stems, destroying entire plants without necessarily eating the whole thing. Up to two inches long, grasshoppers propel themselves with long, strong back legs.

Protect tender seedlings from grasshopper damage with Agronet™ or cheese cloth. Numerous birds, insects, snakes, and toads prey on grasshoppers. Spiders also snare large numbers of grasshoppers in their webs. Rodents, squirrels, mice, and voles eat grasshoppers and their eggs.

Control with hot pepper, soap sprays or sabadilla.

Leafhoppers are small, eighth-inch-long, wedge-shaped insects that are green, white, or yellow. All sap sucking leafhoppers have wings shaped like a peaked roof when they are at rest.

Control leafhoppers by covering plants with Agronet™ or spray with sabadilla or pyrethrum.

Adult **leafminers** lay eggs that hatch into eighth-inch-long green or black maggots that burrow between leaf surfaces, leaving a telltale white tunnel outline. Damage is seldom fatal but can cause reduced harvests.

Ladybugs and lacewings eat leafminer eggs. Unless the infestation is severe, you can remove and destroy infested foliage and the plants will recover.

Mealybugs and scale are most common in warm areas. They look like small raised spots or bits of cotton one eighth- to one quarter-inch long on stems and leaf undersides. They range in color from dark to light.

Lacewings, Australian ladybird beetles, a small mealybug destroyer beetle and Parasitic chalcid wasps are natural predators. They are another natural enemy of several species of mealybugs.

Control by flushing from foliage with cold water. Use a toothbrush or cotton swab dipped in mineral oil or rubbing alcohol to kill small amounts, or use insecticidal soap on infestations.

Slugs and snails are soft, slimy mollusks that hide by day and feed at night. Slugs look like snails without shells. They will eat almost any vegetation, roots included, leaving a slimy trail of silvery mucus in their wake. These creatures winter over in warm, damp locations in most climates. They reproduce prolifically and the young mollusks often eat relatively more than adults. Slugs and snails especially like tender seedlings. They will migrate to adjacent gardens in quest of food. A clean, dry perimeter around the garden will make it difficult for them to pass.

Control large slugs and snails by handpicking. Kill tiny ones with a spray containing a 50 percent ammonia/water solution. When sprayed sparingly, the solution dissolves mollusks without harming the plants.

A thin layer of lime, diatomaceous earth or salty beach sand 2 to 6 inches wide around individual plants, beds or the entire garden will present an impassable barrier to slugs and snails. To trap slugs and snails, attach short one-inch feet on a wide board and leave it in the garden. The pests will seek refuge under the board. Just pick up the board every day or two and shake the slugs off. Step on them, feed them to the chickens, or cut them in two and add to the compost pile as a source of nitrogen.

To make a slug and snail hotel, cut a slot about an inch high and three inches long near the base of a can with a removable lid. Add a little beer, yeast dissolved in water, a jam and water mix or commercial slug/snail bait. The lid prevents rain damage and evaporation, it also discourages birds and animals from eating the mix. Set the slot or door of the hotel near the soil line. The slugs and snails enter at night for a food orgy only to drown. Remove the lid and pour the dead slugs into the compost pile.

Spider mites are range in color from green and yellow to red and have eight legs which distinguish them from six-legged insects. A magnifying glass or low power microscope helps to identify the yellow, white, two spotted, brown, or red mites and their light colored eggs.

Commonly found on house plants and outdoor pot plants in warm climates, spider mites thrive in warm, dry conditions. They pierce leaves and suck out plant juices, leaving small yellowish-white spots on leaves (stippling). These spots are the telltale signs that spider mites are hiding on leaf undersides. If infestation is severe, tiny webs appear between leaves and stems. Misting plants with water makes webs easy to see.

Control by blasting mites off foliage with a jet of cold water. Pay particular attention to the undersides of leaves. If infestation is severe, use insecticidal soap, or a mild lime or pyrethrum spray.

Thrips are tiny, winged, flying insects that rasp on leaves and flower buds, sucking the plant juices for food. Look for distorted leaves that turn pale before dying. Heavily infested plants may have brown or silver leaves with spots. Thrips often occur in the same places as aphids and whiteflies.

Lacewings prey on thrips. Treat infestations with insecticidal soap, dilute oil sprays or rotenone.

Whiteflies are most common in greenhouses and warm climates where they overwinter. To identify, shake the foliage of infested plants and watch for little bright white spots that flicker around and settle back on foliage.

Predators which eat whitefly eggs include parasitic wasp, encarsia formosa, ladybugs and lacewings.

Control with sticky yellow traps (white flies are attracted to the color yellow) hung or placed near infested areas. Ryania, oil, and insecticidal soap are also effective against white flies. (See also leafhoppers)

Fungus

Fungus reproduces by spreading tiny microscopic spores rather than seeds. Many fungi spores are present in the air at all times. With proper conditions, these spores settle and start growing. Unsterile, soggy soil, coupled with humid, stagnant air provides the environment most fungi need to thrive. Although there are many different types of fungi, they are usually treated by the same methods.

Prevention

Cleanliness helps prevent fungus. Dank, ill kept gardens in damp areas with little or no air circulation are most prone to fungi problems.

Once started, fungus can spread like wildfire. Spraying is necessary if the fungus gets a good start and appears to be spreading, even though preventative measures have been taken.

Plant Diseases

Plant diseases are caused by bacteria, fungus, virus, other parasites or growth-inhibiting environmental conditions. Prevent diseases by avoiding conditions that cause them.

Plant diseases are caused or encouraged by poor drainage, poor or imbalanced soil fertility, inadequate air circulation, insect damage and unsanitary conditions.

Soil infertility and poor drainage are normally indicated by sickly plants that are prone to disease and insect attack. Throwing more fertilizers at the soil and trying to control pests on sickly plants may cause more trouble. In the case of poor soil, it is generally better to remove the sickly plants, build the soil and start over with new, healthy plants.

Living soil is full of natural substances that work to keep plants and soils free of disease. Rich, healthy organic soil is one of the best forms of insurance you can have against plant diseases.

Soil-borne diseases tend to accumulate if the soil is planted year after year with the same crop. If possible, let planting holes lay fallow a year or two between plantings.

Plant diseases are more difficult to identify than insect attacks. They may start inside the plant or attack the roots and give little or no notice before killing plants. Other diseases, such as gray mold or rust, do show externally on foliage. They are much easier to identify and control.

Molds, yeasts, and mushrooms are all funguses. They reproduce by means of tiny spores which spread in the air. The best organic way to cope with fungal diseases in the garden is prevention by keeping the garden clean and using good cultural practices. If the disease is so severe that you decide to use a fungicide, identify the disease, choose the least toxic fungicide and use all appropriate safety precautions.

Bacterial diseases are caused by primitive one-celled plants called bacteria. A disease caused by a bacterium will be more difficult to diagnose than one caused by a fungus.

Viruses, too small to be seen with a microscope, also cause plant diseases. They often are carried from plant to plant by other organisms, or by vectors such as insects, mites, or nematodes.

Some conditions that look like diseases are caused not by a fungus, bacterium, or virus but by the culture, the care you are providing.

Blight is a general term that describes many plant diseases. Signs of blight include dark blotches on foliage, slow growth, sudden wilting and plant death. Most blights spread quickly through large areas of plants. Avoid blights by maintaining the proper nutrient balance in the soil, and supply good drainage.

Use a Bordeaux mix (lime/copper sulfate) to control fungal blights. However, the only solution to stopping many blights in their advanced stages, especially those caused by bacteria, is to remove the plants and start over by tilling the soil deeply and amending it with compost to improve drainage. Choose disease-resistant plants whenever possible.

Damping-off is a soil-born fungal disease that attacks young seedlings, cuttings, and transplants at the soil line. The base of the infected stem rots where it meets the soil, or just below the soil line.

Prevent damping-off by providing good air circulation for seedlings, cuttings, or transplants. Make sure the soil drains freely and is damp but not soggy. Many seed companies treat seeds susceptible to damping-off with a chemical fungicide such as Captan.

Avoid damping-off by using a sterile, well-draining mix for growing seeds. After sowing your seeds, sprinkle a light layer of sphagnum peat moss over the top of the planting medium. Sphagnum moss has fungicidal properties.

Downy (false) mildew shows up on leaves, creating pale patches. **Powdery mildew** is a fine pale gray powdery coating on buds, growing shoots and leaves. Mildews cause foliage to yellow and growth to slow. Powdery mildew is limited to the surface of foliage. Downy mildew enters the plants system, growing outward, and is fatal. Powdery mildew is at its worst when roots dry out and foliage is moist. It can be fatal.

Prevent mildews by avoiding cool, damp and humid locations. Mulch the soil and keep foliage dry when watering to keep disease-causing conditions in check. Fungi like dark, moist places.

Control mildews by spraying with Bordeaux mixture (lime/copper sulfate) or dilute baking soda. If the condition is severe, remove the infected foliage and compost or destroy it. Often a combination of both methods is necessary for control.

Bud or gray mold (botrytis) is a crippling fungus that attacks dense buds. This fast growing grayish mold attacks thick buds at the stem. The first signs of botrytis are motley brown splotches that progress to a furry gray mold. Botrytis prospers under cool, damp conditions. Gray mold can spread through the entire garden in a few days.

Prevent gray mold by growing varieties that have sparse buds and providing plenty of air circulation. Avoid over-watering and over-fertilizing with nitrogen. Mulch that stays soggy and damp in shady areas promotes gray mold and should be avoided. Control by pruning and destroying infected growth.

Humid geographic areas with an outside humidity over 70 percent present the biggest problem to fungus control. Bud mold may be triggered when dead foliage rots. When removing yellow leaves between dense buds, pluck the entire leaf and stem so no foliage is left to rot.

Control gray mold by removing the infected bud immediately. Cut out all of the bud mold by removing 2 - 4" below the mold. Keep the bud from contaminating other buds. Wash your tools with alcohol after removing it. There is no chemical or spray that is effective against gray mold.

Leaf spot is the name given to many diseases caused by bacteria, fungi, or nematodes. Black motley spots form on foliage. It is most common in moist, humid garden climates. Excessive watering and lack of air circulation promotes fungal leaf spots. Affected leaves wither and drop.

Prevent fungal leaf spots with adequate air circulation. Control infected foliage by removing and destroying it. If the infection is severe, spot-treat with a fungicide. Sulfur-based fungicides are the least toxic.

Large Pests

Deer and elk can become a problem in locations and seasons where there is little tender natural foliage for them to eat. One grower pees around his patch to keep browsing deer away. You can also surround each plant or the garden with rigid chicken wire. Large pests can also trample plants.

Deer may be repelled by the smell of blood and human hair. Place handfuls of dried blood meal in cloth sacks and dip them in water every few days to activate the smell. Hang the sacks from a tree to discourage dogs and other predators from eating them.

Put handfuls of human hair in small cloth sacks and hang them from a garden fence. Use hair collected at the barber shop. Your hair could be linked to you by the police!!

Mice and voles are normally not much of a problem in the garden. They may become a problem if they chew bark from around the base of plants (girdling). Keep mulch a foot away from trunks if mice are a problem. You can also band the plants with a stiff collar made from plastic or even metal to protect plants from gnawing rodents.

The best mouse deterrent is a cat that is serious about hunting. Mouse traps also work well on smaller populations, but removing a large number of mice with traps can be tedious.

Rabbits eat almost anything in the garden, and multiply, too. Cute little cottontails are most common in urban areas. Their larger cousin, the jackrabbit, inhabits rural areas from Kansas, West.

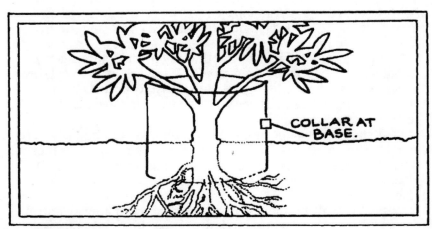

A collar protects the stem from gnawing rodents.

Repel rabbits with a light dusting of rock phosphate on young leaves or dried blood sprinkled around the base of plants. A cow manure tea sprayed on leaves and the soil also may keep them from dining on crops. Rabbits find plants dusted with hot pepper or a spray of dilute fish emulsion and bone meal repulsive. There also are a number of commercial rabbit repellents, but be wary of using these on consumable marijuana.

A dog will help keep rabbits in check, but the only surefire way to keep them out of the garden is to fence them out with one-inch poultry wire. The poultry wire should be buried at least six inches in the ground to prevent burrowing and rise two or three feet above ground.

About Spraying

Use only insecticides and fungicides that are contact sprays for use on edible fruits and vegetables. Read the entire label to find the toxic or active life of the spray. Wait a few more days than the label recommends and thoroughly wash any foliage before ingesting it.

Organic or natural based sprays are also toxic and should be used sparingly. However, sprays such as pyrethrum and insecticidal soaps are not harmful to humans and animals.

Use a respirator or face mask when spraying.

Plastic sprayers do not corrode or rust. Brass nozzle parts with rubber gaskets are easily cleaned with a paper clip. A small, one or two quart spray bottle is easy to carry.

Always wash bottle and pump thoroughly before and after each use.

Mix pesticides or fungicides just before using. When finished spraying, empty the excess spray. Do not use the same mixed spray another day.

Spray early in the day when the temperature is below 70 degrees F. If sprayed just a few hours before nightfall, moisture left overnight on the leaves could cause fungus or water spots.

A plant suffers less shock from the killing spray when more water is in their system. When foliar feeding the garden with a soluble fertilizer, the opposite is true. Plants will absorb the soluble nutrients more rapidly when there is less moisture in the plant and soil.

Have an accurate measuring cup and spoon that are only used for the garden. Keep them clean.

Spray vegetative growth so sprays totally break-down before harvest. Do not spray with toxic chemicals during the last two weeks prior to harvest. If this water is allowed to remain in the flower top a day or longer, mold will find a new home.

Conversion to Metric

When You Know	Multiply By	To Find
Length		
millimeters	0.04	inches
centimeters	0.39	inches
meters	3.28	feet
kilometers	0.62	miles
inches	25.40	millimeters
inches	2.54	centimeters
feet	30.48	centimeters
yards	0.91	meters
miles	1.16	kilometers
Area		
sq. centimeters	0.16	square inches
square meters	1.20	square yards
sq. kilometers	0.39	square miles
hectares	2.47	acres
square inches	6.45	sq. centimeters
square feet	0.09	square meters
square yards	0.84	square meters
square miles	2.60	sq. kilometers
acres	0.40	hectares
Volume		
milliliters	0.20	teaspoons
milliliters	0.60	tablespoons
milliliters	0.03	fluid ounces
liters	4.23	cups
liters	2.12	pints
liters	1.06	quarts
liters	0.26	gallons
cubic meters	35.32	cubic feet
cubic meters	1.35	cubic yards
teaspoons	4.93	milliliters
tablespoons	14.78	milliliters
fluid ounces	29.57	milliliters
cups	0.24	liters
pints	0.47	liters
quarts	0.95	liters
gallons	3.790	liters
Mass and Weight		
grams	0.035	ounces
kilograms	2.21	pounds
ounces	28.35	grams
pounds	0.45	kilograms

Lengths
1 inch (in.) = 25.4 millimeters (mm)
1 foot (12 in.) = 0.3048 meters (m)
1 yard (3 ft) = 0.9144 meters
1 mile = 1.60937 kilometers
1 square inch = 645 square millimeters
1 square foot = 0.0929 square meters
1 square yard = 0.8361 square meters
1 square mile = 2.59 square kilometers

Liquid Measure Conversion
1 pint (UK) = 0.56824 liters
1 pint dry (US) = 0.55059 liters
1 pint liquid (US) = 0.47316 liters
1 gallon (UK) (8 pints) = 4.5459 liters
1 gallon dry (US) = 4.4047 liters
1 pint liquid (US) = 3.7853 liters
1 ounce = 28.3495 grams
1 pound (16 oz.) = 0.453592 kilograms
1 gram = 15.4325 grains
1 kilogram = 2.2046223 pounds
1 millimeter = 0.03937014 inches (UK)
1 millimeter = 0.03937 inches (US)
1 centimeter = 0.3937014 inches (UK)
1 centimeter = 0.3937 inches (US)
1 meter = 3.280845 feet (UK)
1 meter = 3.280833 feet (US)
1 kilometer = 0.6213722 miles

Celsius to Fahrenheit
Celsius temp. x 1.8, +32 = Fahrenheit
Fahrenheit temp. -32, x .55 = Celsius

Light Conversion
1 foot-candle = 10.76 = Lux
1 Lux = 0.09293
Lux = 1 lumen/square meters

INDEX

MARIJUANA OUTDOORS: **GUERILLA GROWING**